Born on 30 May 1903, Father Thomas
Corbishley was educated at the Catholic
College, Preston and Campion Hall, Oxford
(1st in Mods; 1st in Greats). He entered the
Society of Jesus in 1919 and was ordained
priest in 1936. He returned to Campion Hall
as Master in 1945 where he remained until
1958. He was Superior at Farm Street Church
in London from 1958 to 1966. Among his
many publications are: *Agnosticism* (1936),
The Divine Majesty (Tr. 1948) and *The Contemporary Christian* (1966). He also contributes
to many leading journals.

THE SPIRITUALITY OF TEILHARD DE CHARDIN

Thomas Corbishley, S.J.

COLLINS
*The Fontana Library
of Theology and Philosophy*

First published in the Fontana Library 1971
Second Impression September 1971
Third Impression August 1974

© 1971 Thomas Corbishley, S.J.

Printed in Great Britain
Collins Clear-Type Press
London and Glasgow

CONTENTS

I

Introductory

I

SPIRITUALITY

The Teilhardian revolution—it is nothing less—in so much of our thinking finds its truest and most significant expression in the whole field of what we traditionally refer to as 'spirituality'. There is a whole list of terms—the 'spiritual life', 'spiritual' reading, a 'spiritual' outlook—the conventional clichés of the cloister, the pulpit, the convent-parlour, which perpetuate the notion of something esoteric, private, exclusive, associated with a small group of practitioners, set apart from the generality of men. For Teilhard this is an utter falsification of the true position. Since, for him, spirit is ultimate reality, a 'spiritual' outlook is the only authentic outlook; all life, at the human level, is 'spiritual' life or it is, quite literally, meaningless.

Leaving to one side, then, for the present, the traditional interpretation of the word, let us try to see how Teilhard de Chardin understood the word 'spirituality'. He devotes a whole essay to what he calls, typically, 'The Phenomenon of Spirituality'.[1] It will be seen that his application of the idea is far wider than that which it usually bears, but some understanding of his thinking

1. Written in March 1937. See *Human Energy* (Collins, London, 1969), pp. 93 ff.

on the subject is vital to any further study of the more restricted sense of the term.

He begins by pointing out that, since bodies are not only warm, coloured, heavy and so on but also, in certain cases, conscious, the phenomenon of *spirituality* is just as real and *natural* as are the phenomena of heat, light and other physical characteristics. Unfortunately, two opposing attitudes have prevented an adequate appreciation of the meaning of this particular phenomenon. On the one hand, the 'heirs to almost all the spiritualist philosophies of former times' have tended to think of spirit as something so special and lofty that, for all its association with material realities, it cannot be thought of as really belonging to the same world. For them, it is a 'meta-phenomenon'. On the other hand, the materialist thinks of spirit as so frail and limited as to seem almost accidental and certainly secondary. For him, the sole reality is that which can be weighed and measured. Spirit is an 'epi-phenomenon'.

Teilhard then proceeds to develop his own view, refusing to see spirit as either meta-phenomenon or epi-phenomenon. Rather must it be seen as that higher state assumed by the very stuff of the universe. It is true that, at first sight, 'the conscious portion of the world presents itself in the form of discontinuous, tiny and ephemeral fragments: a bright dust of individualities, a flight of shooting stars'.[2] But this is too superficial and partial a view. The more we look at the facts, the more clearly do we see that the purely atomic interpretation of reality is totally inadequate. Certainly, as far as mankind is concerned, a whole network of interconnected forces operates to keep the human species in being; and that

2. Ibid., p. 94.

network becomes more and more complicated, the greater man's own cultural development becomes.

At this stage in his argument, Teilhard takes a step forward, makes a leap which is of doubtful scientific value.

> . . . conscious beings are in truth only different local manifestations of a mass which contains them all. To the extent that it is subject to experiment, the phenomenon of spirit is not a divided mass; it displays a general manner of being, a collective state peculiar to our world.[3]

The scientist will, of course, question the very qualification: 'to the extent that it is subject to experiment'. He will admit that the psychological factors which link human beings together can be studied; he will, as a sociologist, recognize the validity of certain studies within his field; the economist, the political scientist, even the biologist will accept that it is possible to institute investigations into the conduct and the conditions of life throughout the inhabited planet. To what extent can such research produce experimental evidence for the existence of a reality such as Teilhard seems to postulate when he talks about the phenomenon of *spirit*, 'physically defined by a certain tension of consciousness on the surface of the earth'?[4]

The question is fundamental not only to an appreciation of Teilhard's contribution to our present study but also to our attitude to his work taken as a whole. For we have here a crucial example of his habit of extrapolating from a purely scientific and empirical position to a view which seems to go far beyond the hard evidence. Is there, in fact, any justification for such a

3. Ibid., p. 95.   4. Ibid.

leap? Teilhard would probably claim that our scepticism is purely the result of our materialistic preconceptions. What we look for when he talks about a network of interconnected forces is something like the pattern of iron filings which discloses the presence of a magnetic field, or something like the ether which the scientist postulates to explain such phenomena as the propagation of electric impulses or the transmission of light. Surely, he might urge, it is necessary to recognize that, although we cannot see an object without the reflection or refraction of light-waves borne by the ether, the actual event of seeing is of a different order of things from its purely material concomitants. In the same way, though human beings are able to communicate with one another only through some physical medium—talking, reading, touching—the sheer possibility of communication implies the presence of something different from and deeper than these merely external activities. It is the fact that each of us is a *spiritual* being which makes communication between myself and another human being something more than the mere interaction of sound-waves and an ear-drum, of light-waves and a retina.

In other words, just as the physical laws controlling molecular activity are a precondition for any sort of material process, so must there be some analogous set of spiritual laws controlling human intercourse at the intellectual or moral level. It would seem to be this sort of situation which he is attempting to describe when he talks about 'a certain tension of consciousness'. To be specific: a man walking along a country road can see a light in a window, not merely because there is such a light and he himself has eyes, but because of the general situation which makes vision possible. Similarly, if he goes up, knocks on the door and addresses the person who opens it, he might just as well be talking to a brick wall, as we say, unless the conditions are right for communication to be possible. This means much more than the possession of a common language, the ability to speak and to hear, the absence of interference from excessive noise. It means the right psychological climate, for one thing, the sheer willingness to listen and the like. But it demands, at a still deeper level, the presence of that indefinable, indescribable but yet wholly real factor, human consciousness.

Such human consciousness is not just a feature of the two individuals concerned. There could be no human encounter unless there were some sort of link between them, a link *of the same nature* as that which we call human consciousness. This is what Teilhard would have us understand as 'spirit'. It is a present fact, recognizable in my own consciousness, recognizable, by a natural transference, in another's consciousness, postulated as the necessary ground of intercommunication, as necessary as the ether postulated by the physical scientist, though of a different nature. Verified in the individual, it yet transcends all individual limitation.

Nor is spirituality (the quality of being spiritual) 'a recent accident arbitrarily or fortuitously imposed' on the world around us. As we study the long history of man's development, we can see that this is inextricably involved with the onward movement of some force which is other than the mere ebb and flow of material particles. What we call 'matter' moves, changes, develops, becomes transformed under the influence of some inward quality without which it would remain inert and sterile.

The phenomenon of spirit is not therefore a sort of brief flash in the night; it reveals a gradual and systematic passage from the unconscious to the conscious, and from the conscious to the self-conscious. It is a cosmic change of state.[5]

Hence the curious paradox to be found in the relationship between spirit and matter.

In a sense they are both fundamentally the same thing as our modern materialists allege; but between them lies a point of deflection which makes them in some way opposed to each other, as the ancient spiritualists maintained.[6]

Not merely man himself, then, but the whole universe can be understood only in terms of a growing spiritualization. It is true that, parallel to, a kind of obverse of, the forward movement of spirit, there is a negative, destructive dissipation of energy. But it is the positive, constructive, synthesizing power of the spirit which is the more significant, since, without it, even the destructive process would be impossible. This movement of spirit, the sheer tendency to develop, is the story of the cosmos. On it everything depends: nothing can explain it. It is an ultimate.

Moreover, this onward thrust of spirit is irresistible, not in the sense that it nowhere encounters obstacles, checks, frustrations, but in the sense that its direction is set. In the end it must prevail. Unlike purely physical processes such as fall under the scrutiny of the physical sciences, there seems to be no limit to the potential magnitude of spirit. Elsewhere Teilhard introduces a

5. Ibid., pp. 96-7.
6. Ibid., p. 97. By 'spiritualists' Teilhard means those who saw some necessary opposition between spirit and matter.

quotation from Pascal which may serve to illuminate his meaning here.

> The series of men may be considered as a single man, living for ever and continuously learning.[7]

Or, as he himself says,

> *historically*, consciousness on earth has never ceased to expand.[8]

By this he presumably means not merely that more and more human beings have in fact come into existence but also that human knowledge has grown in extent, human power over the resources of the earth has increased enormously, human idealism, human sensitivity (despite appalling lapses) has become more and more elevated. Irresistible and irreversible, spirit is destined of its very nature to take over more and more of the universe.

Yet this process can be halted temporarily, or at least slowed down, since it operates not blindly but through those individual centres of consciousness we call persons. The very fact that human personality emerged from the general evolutionary stream 'so scrupulously prepared over so long a time that nothing quivers when it appears in nature', may lead men to overlook the uniqueness of the human spirit.

> But in reality man marks nothing less than the origin of a new era in the history of the earth. In him for the first time . . . the universe has become conscious of itself, *personalized* . . . The phenomenon of spirit has entered into a higher and decisive phase by becoming the phenomenon of man.[9]

With the entry of the human spirit of man on the stage of the cosmos, a new factor calls for consideration—the moral factor. In an important analysis of this aspect of

7. Ibid., p. 169.   8. Ibid., p. 99.   9. Ibid., p. 102.

his subject, Teilhard distinguishes what he calls the 'morality of balance' from the 'morality of movement'. Laying down the principle that the world is ultimately constructed by moral forces, so that, reciprocally, the function of morality is to construct the world, he pleads for a fresh approach to the whole subject. Morality as it has previously been thought of has been seen as a 'fixed system of rights and duties', aimed at establishing a static equilibrium between man and man. Such an idea rests ultimately on the view of man as a sort of absolute term in the world. Once we come to see him, as we should, as an element destined to fulfil himself, to perfect himself in and through his association with others in a consciousness that transcends, even whilst it includes, his individuality, we shall come to see that a static, undeveloping 'morality of balance' is insufficient. It must be replaced by a morality which is, so to say, open ended, looking forward to a goal yet to be realized, a perfection to be achieved not by an insistence on simple rights and duties based on the existing situation in the world.

The test of the morality of an action will be the degree to which it promotes the growth of spirit. Thus, whilst traditional morality in the sphere of finance contented itself with ensuring fairness in business transactions and the like—'so much for so much'—we must bring ourselves to recognize that the use of riches will be good only in so far as they are put to work for the benefit of the spirit. So with married love.

The morality of love was satisfied by the material founding of a family, love itself being considered a secondary attraction subordinate to procreation. It must now consider as its fundamental object to give

that love just the incalculable spiritual power that it
is capable of developing between husband and wife.[10]

Finally, the implications of such a morality of movement
will necessarily entail belief in a divine being.

A morality of balance may logically be agnostic and
engrossed in possession of the present moment. A
morality of movement necessarily inclines towards
the future, in pursuit of a God,[11]

since such a morality is defined by relation to, directed
towards some future state, a goal which must 'shine
with enough light to be desired and held in view'.

In one of those aphorisms which were responsible for
much of the condemnation uttered against him by
hostile critics, and which need to be clarified in the
light of his general position, he describes 'the God we are
seeking':

a universal God to be realized by effort, and yet a
personal God to be submitted to in love.[12]

The God 'to be realized' is not, of course, to be thought
of as some being in process of development. Rather
must we think of 'realizing' him in the sense that we
make him more and more real *to ourselves*, by our
constant effort towards that ideal which he is in himself, an ideal that is a present actuality. It is the love of
this ideal, perhaps dimly envisaged at first, but becoming
clearer and brighter as we strive towards it, which is
the mainspring and controlling force of our conduct.

The time has passed in which God could simply
impose himself on us from without, as master and
owner of the estate. Henceforth the world will kneel
only before the organic centre of its evolution.[13]

10. Ibid., p. 107.   11. Ibid., p. 109.
12. Ibid.   13. Ibid., p. 110.

The very next sentence seems to be almost an irrelevancy in the immediate context. The fact that Teilhard could introduce it at this stage is an indication that it was, for him, an abiding preoccupation.

> What we are all more or less lacking at this moment is a new definition of holiness.[14]

2

THE PROBLEM

What we are all more or less lacking at this moment is a new definition of holiness.

It may seem a surprising claim to make but it is certainly a valid one to affirm that the chief interest that Teilhard de Chardin had throughout his life was to develop an authentic Christian spirituality. The claim is indeed surprising only to those who have a narrow and partial and one-sided appreciation of the meaning of the word. The best way to approach the spiritual teaching of this great Christian is through an attempt, however brief and sketchy, to outline the history of what we call Christian spirituality.

The central belief of all Christians, whatever their differing interpretations of that belief may be, is that in the Incarnation, God and man, spirit and matter, creator and creature, the supernatural and the natural are fused together in a perfect unity. In theory and in principle, therefore, Christianity is opposed to any sort

14. Ibid.

of dualism, any idea that spirit and matter are antithetical to one another. From the beginning the Church rejected the teaching of Gnostics and Manichees who found some necessary conflict between two ultimate principles: light, spirit, good on the one hand and dark, matter, evil on the other. This world of our human experience is, on this view, the result of some contamination of spirit by matter. On the traditional Judaic view, as formulated in the book of Genesis, God created the world and 'saw that it was good'. This latter view, accepted by the Church, was reinforced by the conviction that Jesus of Nazareth, born of a human mother, was yet the very embodiment of the eternal God.

Such was and remains the official teaching of the Church. Yet, in practice, almost from the beginning of her history an almost contradictory idea has come to prevail. Far too many Christians have believed or at least behaved as if they believed that God's world is somehow at odds with its creator. They have followed Pythagoras and Plato rather than Christ in supposing that the soul is imprisoned in the body and that perfection is to be achieved by the constant attempt to liberate the 'higher and nobler' element in man from the envelope of flesh, seen as an obstacle to true sanctity. Following a Stoic rather than a Christian ideal they have regarded sensitivity to suffering and indeed any kind of emotional reaction as regrettable and to be overcome. They see Nature as the enemy rather than as the vehicle of the supernatural, the natural virtues as not worthy of the name virtue. They are seen by the humanist, and not without justification, as 'sitting loose to civilization'.

The history of this development is highly relevant to our present study. It begins with the problem raised by Christ's own involvement in a complex human situation. Coming as he did to fulfil the destiny of the Jewish nation, preaching a religious ideal which, without rejecting, must yet transcend the Torah, he found himself at variance with orthodox Jewry no less than with the secular authority of Herod in Galilee and Pilate in Judaea. Whilst recognizing the rights of Caesar, he insisted on the paramount rights of God. Extremists, both of the right and of the left, amongst his own people refused to listen to him. Hence the conflict between the 'world' and the followers of Christ. This was heightened by the growing belief that the end of the world was at hand, that it was the Christian's duty to use the world with some reserve, 'because the world as we know it is passing away'.

The reputation which the early Christians had for hating the human race may have sprung from nothing more sinister than a rejection of the ugly features of contemporary pagan civilization. The persecution to which they were subjected at intervals over some two hundred and fifty years can have done little to increase their friendliness towards their fellow-men who were prepared to denounce them to the authorities. A further tendency, the growing practice of taking refuge in the deserts of Syria and Egypt to pursue in solitude that Christian perfection which, it was felt, could not be achieved in the 'worldly' atmosphere of the larger cities and towns, had an effect on Christian ascetic teaching and conduct which has been little short of disastrous. For it set up a kind of ideal Christian community which was, by its very definition, apart from ordinary life. By the Middle Ages, it had become the more or less accepted thing that it was only in monasteries and convents that you would find the Christian life being lived as it should be lived. It was even doubted, at times, whether the layman could achieve salvation. The very involvement in the day-to-day business of looking after a family, a farm, a business concern or whatever it might be was, at the very least, a distraction and, all too probably, a complete impediment to the only thing that mattered, the 'one thing necessary', the 'life of perfection', which meant regulating one's conduct by the Christian 'counsels'—poverty, chastity and obedience. The poor layman had to content himself with the 'life of the precepts', with keeping the commandments, with a sort of second-best Christianity. It is sometimes difficult to remember that, after all, the laity do constitute considerably more than ninety-nine per cent of the total Christian population.

It is true that a work like *Piers Plowman*, with its appeal to the simple toiler and its criticisms of the clergy, provides evidence that the cloister was not universally thought of as the sole harbour of Christian idealism, just as, at a later date, Francis de Sales was writing his *Introduction to the Devout Life* for the benefit of lay people 'striving after perfection'. Yet the whole tendency of 'spiritual writing' has been to emphasize the importance of an 'otherworldliness' that implies much more than a rejection of the 'world' in the pejorative sense of that ambiguous term.

Take, for example, what may be regarded as a classic statement—Thomas Aquinas' definition of 'Christian perfection':

Essentially, the perfection of the Christian life consists

in charity, first and foremost in the love of God, then in the love of the neighbour.[1]

The inevitable conclusion from this sort of language has been, in practice, the notion that we somehow begin by aiming at a love of God 'in himself' and 'then' start at the task of loving our fellow-men. Aquinas meant, of course, an ontological rather than a chronological or even logical sequence; but his interpreters have tended to encourage Christians to make sure that they have arrived at some love of God for his own sake before starting on the extremely risky business of getting involved with their fellow human beings.

Nor is it solely within the Roman Catholic tradition that this sort of mentality was preserved. A quotation from William Law's *A Serious Call to a Devout and Holy Life* may serve to show that the 'traditional attitude' was not much affected by the Reformation.

> He, therefore, is the devout man, who lives no longer to his own will, or the way of the world, but to the sole will of God; who serves God in everything, who makes all the parts of his common life parts of piety, by doing everything in the Name of God, and under such rules as are conformable to His glory.[2]

This statement, like the brief formula of Ignatius Loyola,

> Man has been created to praise, reverence and serve God, and in this way to save his soul,

can be interpreted in a wholly satisfactory sense. But we can understand why such language finds little general acceptance. It is not merely that it gives the unregenerate

1. *Summa Theologica*, IIa IIae, 184, 3.
2. Op. cit., p. 1; Fontana edition, p. 19.

the impression that the devout Christian regards this world as a Slough of Despond, to be struggled through painfully and, of course, disdainfully; it is bound to have a somewhat dehumanizing effect on the well-intentioned believer who tries to take it seriously. Teilhard formulated the problem in this way:

> How can the believer, in the name of everything that is most Christian in him, carry out his duty as a man to the fullest extent and as whole-heartedly and freely as if he were on the direct road to God? ...
>
> The question might be put in this way:
>
> According to the most sacred articles of his *Credo* the Christian believes that life here below is continued in a life of which the joys, the sufferings, the reality, are quite incommensurable with the present conditions of our universe. This contrast and disproportion are enough, by themselves, to rob us of our taste for the world and our interest in it; but to them must be added a positive doctrine of judgement upon, even disdain for, a fallen and vitiated world. 'Perfection consists in detachment; the world around us is vanity and ashes.' The believer is constantly reading or hearing these austere words. How can he reconcile them with that other counsel, usually coming from the same master and in any case written in his heart by nature, that he must be an example unto the Gentiles in devotion to duty, in energy, and even in leadership in all the spheres opened up by man's activity?[3]

What we may call the purely ascetical problem has

3. *Le Milieu Divin* (Collins, London, and Harper & Brothers, New York, 1960), p. 21; Fontana, p. 51; U.S. edition (*The Divine Milieu*), pp. 19-20.

been enormously complicated by the vast changes that have come over the human scene since the main lines of Christian spirituality were laid down. Between the age of Constantine and the end of the fourteenth century it is roughly true to claim that all the major intellectual, artistic, and even scientific developments in Europe and Western Asia had been largely controlled by the Church. (Islamic art and philosophy and Jewish culture are not insignificant exceptions to this generalization, but even they serve to high-light its essential truth.) With the coming of the fifteenth century this ceased to be true. The Renaissance and the 'new learning' meant that scholarship was no longer an ecclesiastical monopoly. The discovery of new continents, despite the great surge of missionary activity which it provoked, meant that the Church ceased to have that predominance in the total world scene as then known which it had had ever since the conversion of the barbarian invaders of Europe. The assault of the Reformers on the whole monastic system meant that the prestige of the cloistered life was seriously impaired. The rise of the great national states and the effective end of the mediaeval concept of the Holy Roman Empire were not without their impact on the authority of the papacy and, in consequence, on certain restraints which the papal court had imposed.

But it was, of course, in the scientific and technological fields that the most significant changes took place—changes that were not merely outside the ambit of ecclesiastical control but were increasingly seen as a challenge to the authority of the Church and, therefore, to the Christian ideal. The Christian *Credo*, based on an over-literal interpretation of the Bible and formulated in terms of an antiquated cosmogony, became more and more perplexing to men who had rejected Aristotelian physics, Ptolemaic astronomy and the general cosmic picture which had dominated men's minds for several millennia.

> The Aristotelian universe was centralized. It had one centre of gravity, one hard core, to which all movement referred. . . . The Copernican universe is not only *expanded* towards the infinite, but at the same time *decentralized*, perplexing, anarchic. . . . The universe has lost its core. It no longer has a heart, but a thousand hearts.[4]

Arthur Koestler's words may seem something of an exaggeration. For most practical purposes, for the vast majority of men, the earth does remain the centre of reference, the sun continues to rise and set, the 'fixed' stars remain fixed. But it is incontestable that a certain conflict did begin to arise in men's minds between the biblical presentation and its 'orthodox' interpretation on the one hand, and the strictly scientific picture on the other. The psychological effect was that religious truth and religious practice came to be seen not as the normal thing, as had been the case until the beginning of the sixteenth century, but rather as in need of justification and defence. A kind of double-think began to invade the minds of believers, an attitude which may best be described by the anecdote of the geology teacher showing a fossil to his class and saying that it was probably so many million years old. 'It must be almost as old as creation itself', said one bright pupil. To which the teacher is reported to have replied: 'Oh, it's much older than that!'

It was not until the nineteenth century that the challenge became really formidable. When it came, it was broadly speaking twofold. On the one hand there was the quite explicit formulation of an evolutionary theory, which seemed to make the world self-perpetuating and self-explanatory, ruling out the accepted view of a 'fixed' creation, even if it was not necessarily opposed to the very notion of creation. A not less significant development was the rise of the whole Marxist teaching, with its emphasis on man's social responsibilities and its rejection of religion as the great obstacle to human progress.

Now it is quite certain that the Christian view of man and of God should have been developing *pari passu* with these intellectual and social movements. The sad fact is that the divisions within Christendom had encouraged believers to think more of the family quarrel and of maintaining certain theological positions rather than to recognize that theology is the servant of truth, not a mere weapon whether of offence or defence. Moreover, and not merely within the Roman Catholic Church, the events of recent centuries—the intellectual and scientific progress of the period from the middle of the fifteenth century to the beginning of the twentieth, the spread of rationalism, the widespread revolt against the *ancien régime* with which the Church had been too closely associated—had engendered a siege mentality, a fear of novelty, a pathetic clinging to traditional formulations of religious beliefs instead of a reshaping of such statements in the light of man's changing vision.

It is relevant in this context to point out that, some fifty years after the publication of the *Origin of Species*,

Teilhard de Chardin was just beginning to discover the
theory and idea of evolution. In his own words:

> I was thirty when I abandoned the antiquated static
> dualism and emerged into a universe in process of
> guided evolution. What an intellectual revolution![5]

But, at a time when the very idea of evolution was
thought to be bound up with a rejection of the idea of
creation, such a conversion was bound to lead to suspicion of unorthodoxy. It was a suspicion which was to
cause his greatest suffering.

3

THE MAN

*I often get the impression that men are now
vegetating, waiting for the appearance of a new
'saint' to give them the lived formula, show them
a practical example of a form of adoration and
perfection that they can vaguely conceive but
cannot formulate for themselves.*[1]

*The saint is the man who Christianizes in himself
all the human of his own time.*[2]

It would, of course, be both misleading and unjust to
give the impression that no Christian before Teilhard

5. Quoted in Henri de Lubac, *The Faith of Teilhard de Chardin*
(Burns & Oates, London, 1965), p. 9.

1. Quoted in Claude Cuénot, *Teilhard de Chardin* (Helicon
Press, Baltimore, and Burns & Oates, London, 1965), p. 403.
2. Ibid.

had grappled with the problem we have been outlining. Already such great Christians as Ernst Troeltsch and Friedrich von Hügel had, from a philosophical and theological standpoint, begun to develop ideas which were strictly in accordance with much that he was to preach. The chief reason why Teilhard would seem to have had a greater and wider impact than either of those two is probably that he was able to write as a scientist with a scientifically trained mind and in close association with other scientists. Perhaps, too, it was his personal history, with its frustrations and disappointments, which ensured that the ground had been privately prepared before the great corpus of his writings was launched on the world. To that history we may now turn.

> There are men who should be recognized as saints for our times, Christians whose faith has impelled them to humanize themselves in every way and to the highest degree.[3]

The words were written by Teilhard de Chardin about a dear friend and colleague. They provide a fitting introduction to this study of his own spiritual development. It is one of the most remarkable features of the life of this most remarkable man that, whilst he could meet the greatest scientists of his day on equal terms, whilst he could and did win the respect and affection of many an unbeliever, his life and his teaching have the most valuable and helpful lessons for all who are concerned to deepen their own spiritual awareness and to understand more fully the meaning of their Christian faith. Much of his language may seem at times to be

3. Ibid., p. 59.

obscure to the point of hiding his meaning; yet there
are many simple, if profound, lessons to be learnt from a
patient study of his writings, and still more from an
understanding of the man himself.

It is, in fact, impossible to appreciate the great lessons
of this inspiring teacher without some knowledge of
his own intellectual and spiritual development. He
was born on 1 May 1881, of a family that was at
once devout, cultured, traditionalist and united by strong
feelings of family affection and French patriotism.
His mother, of whom he himself was to say later that
he owed the best part of what he was, would walk
to morning mass every day before returning home to
take charge of her large household. In all she had
eleven children, of whom Pierre was the fourth. From
her he learnt that devotion to the Sacred Heart which
was to be one of the mainsprings of his spiritual practice.
The family, including the servants and the workmen
on the estate, would meet each evening for prayers before the children went to bed. It was, in many ways, a
typical French family of the lesser nobility. It seemed
improbable that such a setting would produce one of the
geniuses of our century.

There is a precious glimpse of his early days, from
an account written by a cousin, Marguerite Teillard-
Chambon, with whom he was to form a lasting friendship and to whom many of his countless letters were to
be addressed.

These old houses, with their cellar-like entrances, their
huge staircases, cold and damp, and their sombre, lofty
rooms, were a grim setting for our childhood. But
they never stopped us from playing—the 'terrible

quartet' of boys, Albéric, Pierre, Gabriel and Joseph, wild and noisy, the girls more sedate, Françoise, Bernadette, two Maries, two Marguerites.[4]

A large family is the best school for discipline, for unselfish consideration for others, for an authentic humility, since brothers and sisters are the most unsparing critics of each other and easily deflate any pomposity or self-importance. Although the life of Pierre was to take him far from his home in the Auvergne, he never forgot the simple lessons he had learnt there. Of him it might most truly be said that he ever remained 'true to the kindred points of heaven and home'. Yet, already in his very earliest years, he was to show signs of his future concern, almost one might call it his obsession, with the abiding and the absolute. He would collect hard, resistant, unassailable objects. He was saddened to discover that the solidity of iron could be impaired by rust, so he turned to various kinds of stone, crystals of quartz and amethyst, shining fragments of chalcedony—symbols, yet more than symbols; embodiments of the real which was to be his life-long pursuit.

He was hardly eleven when he went to boarding-school, with the Jesuit fathers at Villefranche—the famous Notre-Dame de Mongré, with the punning motto: *Le grè de Dieu mon grè*—'God's will is my will'. He was a pupil of great promise, though he confessed to boredom with the uninspired pieties of religious instruction:

All those goody-goody romances about the saints and

4. Quoted in *Teilhard de Chardin Album*, edited by J. Mortier and M.-L. Auboux (Collins, London, and Harper & Row, New York, 1966), p. 15.

the martyrs! Whatever normal child would want to spend an eternity in such boring company?[5]

It was an early manifestation of an unconventionality of view based not on mere contrariness but on an awareness of a more meaningful underlying truth. That he was both intelligent and hard-working is emphasized by his contemporaries. We also know that at school he developed a strong devotion to Our Lady—a devotion that was to be an abiding inspiration. But here too the devotion was to be no mere subjective 'attitude of mind'; it must be tested in action. In a precious record of an address given by the director of the Sodality of Our Lady, of which at the time Pierre was secretary, the members were encouraged to see that

the best way to show our love for the Blessed Virgin is to try to be men with a sense of duty, that is Christians.[6]

It is hardly surprising that, coming from such a home and educated at such a school, he developed a vocation to the Society of Jesus, becoming a novice in March 1899 when he was not quite eighteen. During the whole of his life henceforward he would be under the influence of the *Spiritual Exercises*, that great instrument of ascetic and religious formation which, after the Bible itself, is the book most familiar to Jesuits. Year after year he would ponder the words of the opening Fundamental Principle:

Man has been created to praise, reverence and serve the Lord his God . . . Everything else on earth has been created for man's sake . . .

5. Quoted in Robert Speaight, *Teilhard de Chardin: A Biography* (Collins, London, 1967), p. 27.
6. C. Cuénot, op. cit., p. 5.

Year after year his retreats would conclude with the famous Contemplation for Achieving Love:

Love should be expressed in doing rather than in protesting. Love consists in a reciprocal inter-change, the lover handing over and sharing with the beloved his possessions . . . Recall the good things I have had from creation . . . See God in his creatures—

in matter, giving it existence,

in plants, giving them life,

in animals, giving them consciousness,

in men, giving them intelligence.

So he lives in me, giving me existence, life, consciousness, intelligence.

More, he makes me his temple . . .

Think of God energizing, as though he were actually at work, in every created reality, in the sky, in matter, plants, and fruits, herds and the like . . .

Realize that all gifts and benefits come from above. My moderate ability comes from the supreme Omnipotence on high, as do my sense of justice, kindliness, charity, mercy, and so on . . . like sunbeams from the sun or streams from their source.

Teilhard de Chardin was to add immeasurably to the content of such ideas; yet there is a sense in which we can see, implicit in such an outline, the themes which he was to develop so vigorously and inspiringly in the half-century and more of his life as a Jesuit. Life in the Society of Jesus was, as we shall see, to bring him frustration and sorrow; yet it was, at the same time, to be the making of him. If his superiors were to show a regrettable timidity in refusing to allow him to publish certain writings which seemed, at the time, dangerously novel, it was these same superiors who encouraged his scientific bent and gave him every opportunity to pursue his interests in the realms of geology, palaeontology, the study of human origins, which were to provide the basis for his larger speculations.

It is unnecessary to follow in any detail the successive stages of his course of training as a Jesuit, though it is important to recall one feature of his intellectual development—the discovery of the idea of evolution. Until the years of his theological studies he was content to accept the traditional view of the creation of 'fixed species'. Now, partly under the influence of his own interest in fossils—an interest that followed on his earliest desire for something permanent, unchanging, absolute—and partly by a reading of Bergson's work on *Creative Evolution*, he became a passionate enthusiast for the theory that had been growing in importance in scientific circles for the last half-century. The very word 'evolution' rang through his thought 'like a refrain, a taste, a promise, a demand'. He saw it as the scientific statement of the deeper theological truth of the divine action in creation.

Although Teilhard had taught for three years in Cairo as a Jesuit scholastic, and, as a young priest, spent some weeks in pastoral work amongst the farmers of the Pas de Calais and the artisans of Paris, he was still largely unaffected by the outside world. But all this was to change dramatically with the outbreak of the 1914 war. In December of that year he was called up (in France priests do not enjoy freedom from military service) and was sent to the Front as stretcher-bearer, attached to a Moroccan regiment. It was to be his 'baptism in the real'[7] to use his own phrase. Here he came up against destruction, suffering and death on a colossal scale. He shared the dangers and discomforts, the fears and frustrations, the squalor and degradation of trench warfare. He came to know human nature in a way that might otherwise have been impossible. His own optimism, his serenity, his faith were to be tested to the limit. He came out of it all enriched and, in a sense, fulfilled.

Astonishingly, during these years of physical danger and mental stress, he was to produce a body of writing in which it is possible to see, not merely in embryo but already well developed, the ideas which he was to spend the rest of his life deepening and preaching. He wrote in a letter on 28 May 1915,

Fundamentally, I'm glad to have been at Ypres. I hope to emerge more of a man and more of a priest.[8]

'More of a man and more of a priest,' for he saw his priestly vocation as a call to enlarge man's vision of his destiny. He had been ordained a priest in 1911—the actual date was 24 August. What his priesthood came to mean to him may best be gathered from two pieces of writing. In July 1918, somewhere between Compiègne and Soissons, he completed an essay in which he outlined his ideas about the role of the priest. In the first section, entitled 'Consecration', he sketched out a moving and inspiring notion which he was to develop

7. Quoted in Emile Rideau, *Teilhard de Chardin: A Guide to his Thought* (Collins, London, 1967), p. 21.
8. *The Making of a Mind* (Collins, London, and Harper & Row, New York, 1965), p. 56.

some five years later in 'The Mass on the World'. Prevented by circumstances from saying mass in the strictly liturgical manner (we need to remember that he was writing at the time of the great advance which was to lead to final victory), he enlarged his vision to take in a fuller view of what the mass really meant.

> Is not the infinite circle of things the one final Host that it is your will to transmute?[9]

There is a sense in which the whole of Teilhard's spiritual teaching is stated in that brief question. For him, the whole of 'religion', centred on the mystery of the Eucharist, expressed in the priest's daily offering of Christ's sacrifice, was itself meaningful only in terms of that larger vision which was able to pierce through to the divine and divinizing activity of the Creator at work throughout the whole vast cosmos.

> The seething cauldron in which the activities of all living and cosmic substance are brewed together—is not that the bitter cup that you seek to sanctify?[10]

Or, as he was to state it some years later in one of his letters,

> It seems to me that in a sense the true substance to be consecrated each day is the world's development during that day—the bread symbolizing appropriately what creation succeeds in producing, the wine (blood) what creation causes to be lost in exhaustion and suffering in the course of its effort.[11]

Yet the priest is ordained not simply to consecrate the elements, to adore and lead others in adoration of God in

9. 'The Priest', *Writings in Time of War* (Collins, London, and Harper & Row, New York, 1968), p. 205.
10. Ibid.
11. *Letters from a Traveller* (Collins, London, and Harper & Row, New York, 1962), p. 86; Fontana, p. 46.

his world, to communicate himself and to administer communion to others; he is also called to be an apostle, to lead others to a deeper understanding of what life means.

> If you judge me worthy, Lord God, I would show to those whose lives are dull and drab the limitless horizon opening out to humble and hidden efforts; for these efforts, if pure in intention, can add to the extension of the incarnate Word a further element —an element *known* to Christ's heart and gathered up into his immortality. . . . And above all, I shall remind those who suffer and mourn that the most direct way of making our life useful is to allow God to grow within us, and, through death, to substitute himself for us.[12]

Yet this man, whose highest ambition was to bring all men, believers and unbelievers, to a realization of what was, for him, the obvious truth, that only in God and in Christ does the object of scientific investigation, the cosmos in all its rich variety, find its explanation and purpose, this man was treated for years as though he was a near-heretic and a danger to Catholic orthodoxy. Whilst his reputation as a scientist grew steadily in professional circles, in Catholic circles, even in the Society of Jesus, he was to be regarded to the day of his death with suspicion and distrust. Explanation for this extraordinary attitude is to be found, of course, in the conservatism which is all too often seen as synonymous with orthodoxy. The Church was still obsessed with the memory of the (largely exaggerated) 'Modernist crisis'. The Jesuit authorities felt it their duty to support

12. 'The Priest', op. cit., pp. 220-1.

the 'traditional line' of the Holy Office. They were doubtless also actuated by a desire to protect Teilhard himself from the possibility of condemnation.

In 1925, as the result of his writing a purely private paper containing speculations about the way in which the doctrine of original sin should be presented in the light of contemporary thinking, he was required to sign a document subscribing to six specific propositions, as a guarantee of his orthodoxy. At the same time, his career as a teacher at the Institut Catholique in Paris was, at the wish of his superiors, terminated. A letter to a Jesuit friend gives some idea of his feelings.

> Dear friend, Please help me. I've put a good face on it outwardly, but within it is something that resembles an agony or a storm. I think I see that, if I separated myself off, or kicked over the traces in any way whatsoever (humanly speaking it would be so simple and so 'easy'), I would be disloyal to my faith in Our Lord's animation of everything that happens . . . It is essential that I should show, by my example, that if my ideas seem innovations, they nevertheless make me as faithful as anyone to the old attitude.[13]

It was not simply his personal feelings that were involved. He was saddened to see the Church he loved unable to speak to the world he loved.

> . . . the only thing that I can be: a voice that repeats, *opportune et importune*, that the Church will waste away so long as she does not escape from the factitious world of verbal theology, of quantitative sacra-

13. Letter to Père Valensin: see *Letters to Léontine Zanta* (Collins, London, and Harper & Row, New York, 1969), p. 30.

mentalism, and over-refined devotions in which she is
enveloped, so as to reincarnate herself in the real
aspirations of mankind. . . . I can't get away from the
evidence that the moment has come when the
Christian impulse should 'save Christ' from the hands
of the clerics so that the world may be saved.[14]

Elsewhere he said

I feel bound, by my very substance, to an organism
whose unwarranted narrowness and irrelevance I am
perpetually aware of.[15]

Nevertheless, the suffering he endured was intense,
though his sense of loyalty to both the Church and the
Society remained unshaken.

I think it is my fate (and perhaps my vocation) to have,
and to suffer from, this consciousness of a leap in the
dark. My greatest comfort is the thought that I have
always done my best to serve the Power that draws us
into itself.[16]

But that service could only be, for him, within the
Church and the Society.

I am conscious of feeling myself fundamentally bound
to both, for new and ever more cogent reasons—by
which I mean that I believe I would be betraying
'the World', if I deserted the post I have been assigned
to. In this sense, I love them both, and I want to
work, as an individual atom, to perfect them *from
within*, with no trace of antagonism. You may be
quite certain that the very idea of taking steps to
leave the Order has never even crossed my mind.[17]

On another occasion he said:

14. Ibid., p. 34-5.   15. Ibid., p. 36.
16. E. Rideau, op. cit., p. 298.   17. Ibid.

. . . nothing spiritual, nothing divine, can reach a
Christian—or a religious save through the intermediary
of the Church—or of his Order.[18]

So he persevered to the end, working at his task as a
scientist, spending years in virtual exile in China, at-
tending conferences in Europe and America, visiting
Africa to study there the evidence for the origins of
mankind. All the time the fire of his enthusiasm, the
light of his vision seem to glow with a greater brightness
and warmth. Yet we know how much he suffered; he
had his share of the sorrows common to those who
lose their dear ones—his eldest brother died not long after
Pierre had taken his first vows as a Jesuit; a younger
sister died two years later at the age of twelve; another sister was a permanent invalid; two more brothers
were killed in the First World War; several of his
closest friends were taken from him; he was no stranger
to that sense of foreboding and insecurity which even the
greatest spirits know.

I am afraid . . . like all my fellow-men, of the future
too heavy with mystery and too wholly new, towards
which time is driving me. Then like these men I
wonder anxiously where life is leading me.[19]

As we have seen he suffered from the hesitations, the
doubts, the lack of trust displayed by his superiors. He
passed through that purifying process which is the
universal experience of all religious souls.

. . . the supernatural awaits and sustains the progress
of our nature. But it must not be forgotten that it

18. *Letters to Léontine Zanta*, p. 37.
19. *Hymn of the Universe* (Collins, London, and Harper &
Row, New York, 1965), p. 30; Fontana, p. 29.

purifies . . . in the end only in an apparent annihilation.[20]

He was no stranger to human love, with all the suffering that, especially in his way of life, this must involve.

One knows oneself, and one is master to some extent of one's own suffering. But what does one know about the forces one may unloose in someone else; forces that one cannot satisfy.[21]

All this is true. Yet the impression he made on those who knew him well was one of peace and serenity, of power and secure faith, of joy and hope. One friend, on first meeting him was impressed by

his long face, forceful and finely drawn; the features, emphasized by premature lines, looked as though carved out of some tough wood. There was a lively twinkle in his eye; humour, too, but no hint of irony; forbearing and kind.[22]

This is how another spoke of him:

A man of unequalled style; of a self-effacing and irresistible distinction. His voice, his diction which had the tone of a harpsichord, his smile which never quite turned to laughter, impressed themselves on anyone who was in the least attentive . . . As simple in his gestures as in his manners . . . You felt that even if you were as tall as he, you were still infinitely far removed from the storehouse of his thoughts which were never inflated. As a rule you stopped dead before that rough-hewn face that Greco had prefigured . . .[23]

He died on Easter Sunday, 1955—towards the end of

20. *Le Milieu Divin*, p. 84; Fontana, p. 101; U.S. ed., p. 76.
21. R. Speaight, op. cit., p. 212.   22. Ibid., p. 141.
23. Ibid., pp. 184-5.

his seventy-fourth year. A few years earlier he had composed this prayer:

Lord of my childhood and Lord of my end—God complete in yourself and yet, for us, ever born anew . . . sweep away at last all the clouds that hide you still—clouds of hostile prejudice and of false belief. And, by what is at once diaphaneity and total conflagration, may your Universal Presence leap forth.[24]

His epitaph might well be the words of the great philosopher, Etienne Gilson: 'Everything in him was pure. Under the continual flow of scientific and other alluvions he kept intact and scrupulously preserved the nugget of pure gold which was the piety and faith of his childhood.'[25]

24. *Le Coeur de la Matière*, 1950 (unpublished).
25. R. Speaight, op. cit., p. 326.

II

The Foundations of Teilhardian Spirituality

We have seen how Teilhard, during his life, was regarded with suspicion as a preacher of dangerous, if not heretical, doctrine. Even after his death, as his works came into wider circulation, hostile critics seized on phrases or isolated sentences and found him guilty of the most bizarre and unorthodox views. Yet, whilst we have to recognize that his at times ambiguous language and his habit of speculating about possible theological developments laid him open to such charges, there is much truth in Gilson's judgement that 'he kept intact . . . the piety and faith of his childhood'. Perhaps the most effective way of bringing home this truth is to show how his spiritual teaching can be classified under a number of quite 'traditional' headings.

In the first section, entitled quite simply 'God', we shall see how he thought of God and how he related all his ideas—scientific, especially, but also psychological and what, for want of a better term, we must call sociological —to that basic truth. The second section, 'Christ', treats of what is the most important and characteristic contribution that Teilhard has made to the spiritual life of the Christian believer. For he was convinced that any genuinely Christian way of living must be grounded not merely in a personal relationship with Jesus of Nazareth, as a historical figure in the remote past, but equally, indeed much more, in a sense of the cosmic Christ, the Christ not merely of the Synoptists but of the Fourth Gospel too and, above all, of St Paul. For them, and therefore for the Christian, Jesus of Nazareth is the incarnate Word of God, in whom and for whom created reality has come into being, in whom and from whom it finds its total meaning.

The third section, 'Mary', develops another characteristically Teilhardian idea, that of a feminine principle running throughout creation, a principle of unification, finding its most authentic expression in the Mother of God, the supreme Woman, and, as a kind of parallel to the cosmic Christ, the Church, which is his Body and his Bride. A final section, 'Fullness of Life', develops Teilhard's plea for an authentic Christian life, based on the argument that the purely negative emphasis on renunciation, which has been such a feature of so much Christian ascetic treatment is not only self-defeating, but is both untrue to the doctrine of the Incarnation and also a great scandal to the unbeliever.

I

GOD

There can be no doubt that we are conscious of carrying within us something greater and more indispensable than ourselves: something that existed before we did and could have continued to exist without us: something in which we live, and that we cannot exhaust: something that serves us but of which we are not masters: something that will gather us up when, through death, we slip away from ourselves and our whole being seems to be evaporating.[1]

The God whom our century awaits must be (1) as vast and mysterious as the cosmos; (2) as immediate as life itself; (3) as bound up with (in some way) our effort as mankind itself.[2]

Every conversation I have ever had with communist intellectuals has left me with a decided impression that Marxist atheism is not absolute, but that it simply rejects an 'extrinsical' God, a deus ex machina *whose existence can only undermine the dignity of the universe and weaken the springs of human endeavour—a 'pseudo-God', in short, whom no one in these days wants, least of all Christians.[3]*

In recent years we have heard much talk about the 'death' of God. Such language is, of course, meaningless if men suggest by it that God once existed but does so no longer. But if we think of it in terms of Teilhard's dictum

God is complete for himself: for us he is continually being born,[4]

we begin to see that it has a profound relation to man's spiritual need. As another great man of our century has said:

1. The Soul of the World', *Writings in Time of War*, p. 181.
2. 'Note pour servir à l'évangilisation des temps nouveaux', 1919.
3. *The Future of Man* (Collins, London, and Harper & Row, New York, 1964), pp. 266-7; Fontana, p. 279.
4. E. Rideau, op. cit., p. 150.

God does not die on the day when we cease to believe
in a personal deity, but we die on the day when
our lives cease to be illumined by the steady radiance,
renewed daily, of a wonder, the source of which is
beyond all reason.[5]

'Beyond all reason'—this is indeed the God we worship.
Yet it remains true—and Teilhard would always insist
on this—that our human experience, not least the
exercise of our reason, brings us inexorably face to
face with such evidences for the existence of God that, if
we are to go on being reasonable, we must make the
final leap of faith, the 'grand option' as he called it in
one of his essays, into a total acceptance of God with
all that that acceptance implies.

For him the universe of our daily encountering, as it
is the object of study for a multitude of scientific dis-
ciplines, must be seen as a vast unity of interlocking
forces, working together to produce ever higher forms
of being, culminating in man. For some men, the fact
that life is known with certainty to exist only on our
planet is an argument for suggesting that it is somehow
accidental, peripheral to the boundless energizing of
the cosmos. Apart from the fact that, by the same line
of argumentation, things like gold and diamonds would
have to be regarded as valueless because purely accidental
products of the vast masses of material that have to
be sifted to discover them, Teilhard says,

The fact that Life is so rarely encountered in the
sidereal immensity is precisely because, representing
a higher form of cosmic evolution, it can only come

5. Dag Hammarskjold, *Markings* (Faber & Faber, London, 1965),
p. 65.

into existence in privileged circumstances of time and place.[6]

Life is, so to say, supported by all the infra-structure of material elements, nuclei, atoms, molecules which have no special significance in their individual existence but become more and more meaningful as they become more and more complex and interconnected.

So the world is arranged and organized for Life and life in its turn reaches a higher level in consciousness and, at length, in that unique form of self-conscious, re-flective awareness which we call reason or intelligence. We recall the words of St Ignatius 'Everything else on the face of the earth has been created for the sake of man . . .' Only Teilhard would not limit the 'face of the earth' to this planet of our solar system. For him the whole vast cosmos itself is for man and, in an important sense, subjected to man. Man exists not simply to profit from the resources of nature but to develop and control those resources for his further advantage.

Teilhard was, of course, already dead when the Russians launched their first sputnik in 1957 and gave the impetus to that exploration of space which reached a dramatic stage when men first set foot on the moon less than twelve years later. But we know what his reaction would have been to these events. His reaction was already recorded over fifty years ago in another of his war-time essays:

Then, is it really true, Lord? By helping on the spread of science and freedom, I can increase the density of the divine atmosphere, in itself as well as for me: that atmosphere in which it is always my own

6. *The Future of Man*, p. 216; Fontana, p. 224.

desire to be immersed. By laying hold of the earth I
enable myself to cling closely to you. . . .

May the kingdom of matter, then, under our
scrutinies and our manipulations, surrender to us the
secrets of its textures, its movements, its history.

May the world's energies, mastered by us, bow
down before us and accept the yoke of our power.

May the race of men, grown to fuller consciousness
and greater strength, become grouped into rich and
happy organisms in which life shall be put to better
use and bring in a hundredfold return.[7]

But this does not mean that man is on earth simply to
live a life of increasing comfort and material well-
being, without regard to anything higher or more noble.
On the contrary, since, as Teilhard maintains, the
evolution of the universe has an absolute direction, which
is towards spirit, it follows that everything in a man's
life must be subordinated to his spiritual quest, to the
fulfilment of his spiritual nature. Above all, man, of
his nature and because of his relationship with the
world about him, cannot avoid the challenge of God's
immediate presence. In a passage of sheer poetry, Teilhard explains what he means:

A limpid sound rises amidst the silence; a trail of pure
colour drifts through the glass; a light glows for
a moment in the depths of the eyes I love . . .

Three things, tiny, fugitive: a song, a sunbeam, a
glance . . .

So, at first, I thought they had entered into me in
order to remain and be lost in me.

7. 'The Mystical Milieu', *Writings in Time of War*, pp. 138-9.

On the contrary: they took possession of me, and bore me away.

For if this plaint of the air, this tinting of the light, this communication of a soul were so tenuous and so fleeting it was only that they might penetrate the more deeply into my being, might pierce through to that final depth where all the faculties of man are so closely bound together as to become a single point. Through the sharp tips of the three arrows which had pierced me the world itself had invaded my being and had drawn me back into itself . . .

The Real incessantly reawakens us to an impassioned awareness of a wider expansion and an all-embracing unity . . . when the world reveals itself to us it draws us into itself: it causes us to flow outwards into something belonging to it, everywhere present in it, and more perfect in it.[8]

The line of his argument is becoming clear. Soon its conclusion is made explicit:

Lord, it is you who, through the imperceptible goadings of sense-beauty, penetrated my heart in order to make its life flow out into yourself. You came down into me by means of a tiny scrap of created reality; and then, suddenly, you unfurled your immensity before my eyes and displayed yourself to me as Universal Being.[9]

These passages occur in an essay which is treating explicitly of mystical experience. At a different level of argumentation he approaches the subject of God's existence as it were negatively. Using what is equivalently the Cartesian method of methodic doubt, he pictures himself as having ceased to believe in Christ, in

8. Ibid., pp. 117-18.   9. Ibid., p. 120.

a personal God, even in the spirit. He could not lose his faith in the world. This is a solid, undeniable, worthwhile reality, possessing its own goodness, even, he says, its own 'infallibility'. To refuse to accept this basic faith is to fall into the madness of solipsism. Therefore, this is the basic conviction which all men share. What are its implications?

First of all, Teilhard would argue, the evidence for an evolutionary process is overwhelming. Moreover, that process manifestly leads to the production of man. Man is the meaning of evolution, in the sense that the whole process has significance not *qua* process but *qua* process-producing-man. Equally, if evolution can be explained solely in terms of man, man in turn can be explained—though not wholly—in terms of evolution. If we are to understand what he is, we can do so only by looking back over the millennia which have succeeded one another, slowly, painfully, yet always moving along an axis that somehow controls and directs the whole fermentation which, from the primeval cosmic stuff, through the emergence of life and consciousness, has resulted in this intelligent being, *Homo sapiens*.

Is this the end of the story? On the contrary, it is, in a sense, only the beginning. For now man himself has become the very principle and guiding force of the evolutionary process. How that process is to continue will depend now on him, on the use he makes of his opportunities, on his wisdom and sense of responsibility. In *The Phenomenon of Man*, in which he tries to outline his understanding of man's place in the cosmos, he describes the world-process as moving towards what he calls point Omega. This he sees as the tip of the cone of evolution, the material base becoming more and more refined as spirit takes over, until in the end the process is complete and man finds his perfection realized for ever.

But here, what at first sight looks like a focus of purely natural development, turns out, after all, to be a transcendent, divine, energizing reality, the necessary condition of the whole process itself.

To put it in other words, point Omega may be looked at in two ways. We may see it either as a point as yet unrealized—an ideal, future state of affairs—or as a present reality. We may see it as the culminating point of the whole time-space process, or as the eternal, ever-active Being drawing that same process onwards towards its fulfilment, which will be realized in him. For, as Teilhard insists over and over again, the whole evolutionary process is meaningless unless it is seen in terms of personal activity and personal achievement. The mere blind collision of impersonal forces has and can have no lasting significance. If evolution has an axis —and if it has not then it will, quite literally, get nowhere—that axis must be the controlling agency of spiritual power. But that controlling spiritual agency, whilst it may be thought of as a development of evolution, is, in turn, itself a reflection of the eternal spirit of God himself. God's creative action is not something that should be thought of as having occurred, once and for all, at the beginning of time; rather must we see it as the all-pervading energizing of God in and through the whole process of cosmic activity.

Not that our awareness of God in his world is in the nature of a direct intuition, like perceiving gravity at work in the falling apple or the magnetic force in the pattern of iron filings.

It cannot . . . be attained directly by any process of
reasoning nor by any human artifice. It is a gift, like
life itself, of which it is undoubtedly the supreme
experimental perfection . . . To experience the attraction of God, to be sensible of the beauty, the consistency
and the final unity of being, is the highest and at
the same time the most complete of our 'passivities of
growth' . . . by the very logic of his creative activity
God tends to make himself sought and perceived
by us . . .[10]

Another analogy may help us. In contemplating a work
of art, listening to a musical composition, reading a
book, our immediate awareness is of the picture, the
melody, the meaning of the passage under our eyes: it
requires a different sort of effort, a reflection on our
experience, to be conscious of the painter, the composer,
the poet. It is through the medium of his work that he
reveals himself to us. So, in the end, the initiative, the
awakening, comes from God; no progress in this
domain is achieved except as a fresh response to a fresh
gift.

Yet God's creative power does not really fashion us as
though out of soft clay. It is a fire that kindles life in
whatever it touches, a quickening spirit. Therefore it
is *by living* that we must decisively adapt ourselves to
it, model ourselves upon it, identify ourselves with it.
Above all, man's response to the creative stimulus of
God's spirit must be in the nature of what Teilhard
calls 'a faith that gets things done' (which seems to be a
better translation than the conventional term 'operative
faith'). Even at the natural level, as he points out, men
are inspired by what he calls a 'natural faith'—the faith

10. *Le Milieu Divin*, p. 122; Fontana, p. 131; U.S. ed., p. 111.

that is professed by those who believe that they have found a way of influencing the future. For, after all, such men are convinced that it is possible to impose some sort of pattern, some regularity upon the future that does not yet exist. Thus, even at this natural level, the man without any religious convictions implicitly recognizes the truth of St Paul's definition of faith as that which gives substance to our hopes. Fortune, we say, favours the brave. Yes, says Teilhard, that is true: but it is not less true that courage conditions chance. 'A line of action pressed on with perseverance seldom fails to create around, and *ahead* of it, a current of favourable events.'[11]

Therefore, in accordance with one of his most fundamental convictions, namely that the natural order of things is a pointer to supernatural truths (since, as St Thomas teaches, although the supernatural falls outside that which is natural, it is yet the end towards which nature is ordered), Teilhard sees the faith of the Christian as involving a similar challenge. In a striking passage he declares:

Fundamentally, the Christian has received from his Saviour the power of mastering fortune: that is to say he can so control the chances as to make them work in his favour. If that were not so, it would be impossible to account for the efficacy of prayer, and the saying *Credenti, omnia convertuntur in bonum* [to him that believes, everything works out for the best] would be meaningless. . . .

The point, however, is this: how is that control realized?[12]

11. 'Operative Faith', *Writings in Time of War*, p. 234.
12. Ibid., p. 238.

In a fascinating analysis, he suggests that we must look at the universe not just as one organic unity, which it is, but also in terms of the individuals units making it up.

> In virtue of some divine foreknowledge which controls the progress of the whole as a function of the freedom of each one, it is just as though there were, in the single event-system that determines the state of the universe at a given moment, as many *independent providences* as there are souls in the world. Thus each one of us has, in reality, *his own* universe: he is its centre and he is called upon to introduce harmony into it, just as though he were *alone 'in rerum natura'* [on the face of nature].
>
> In the light of this 'polyvalence' of the cosmos . . . each one of us, by confident prayer, can modify *his own* future without necessarily interfering with that of his neighbour—without even disturbing, in any *scientifically* demonstrable way, the course of natural events.[13]

Even chance can be seen as compatible with divine providence. It is through chance, just as, at the opposite extreme, it is through man's free choices, that creative power enters into the world by controlling the collective play of secondary causes.

Summing up what he has to say about the achievement brought about through Christian faith, he holds, then, that it in no way destroys or even distorts any individual established fact or way of behaving, since prayer does not normally change events; it integrates them into a new total combination. Nor must we think of the Christian life in terms of natural human achievement; it has to do essentially with growth in holiness. Moreover, it is, in

13. Ibid., pp. 238-9.

the end, God who is at once agent, origin and medium of its effects.

We are here, of course, faced with the obscurities and the paradoxes that have beset man's efforts to try to describe the nature of God and his action in the world. Some have accused Teilhard of having so confused and blended God's action in the universe with the evolutionary process itself as to end up in sheer pantheism—the view, that is, that God is somehow constituted by the elements of the world. It is a notion formally and explicitly rejected by him in more than one passage. God cannot, he says, be intermingled with or lost in the participated being which he sustains and animates and holds together. Indeed a God who was in any way identified with the world would not be worthy of man's worship. No, God is essentially transcendent, complete and perfect in himself, utterly independent of the world-process which he yet guides and inspires. At the same time, he is imminent in that process, since the process itself would be both meaningless and impossible without him. Therefore, the more a man studies, promotes and involves himself in the development of nature, the more clearly does he come to realize the presence of God all about him. It follows, therefore, that the whole scientific revolution of the last century and more, which seems to have blinded men's eyes to the deepest religious truths, ought to be opening them more and more to the sheer fact of God. 'God is becoming manifest to our consciousness as greater and more necessary than ever.'

Why, then, is there this apparent conflict between the scientific and the religious mentality? The reasons are complex, but Teilhard would single out two in particular. It is true, on the one hand, that the sheer achievement of science can so intoxicate the mind with the beauty and wonder of creation that the man of science is tempted to rest there and not pursue the logic of thought right through to the end. 'The earth'—that is the whole body of agnostic thought—'was so absorbed by and took such delight in its earliest conquests, that at first it could only relax in amazement and feel that it lacked nothing.' But 'the yawning void, deep within it, that calls out for the Absolute . . . tried to *forge for itself some Divinity* . . . whose glory would crown and illuminate the endless slope of evolution: omnipotent science, mankind, the superman. Idols all—'[14]

That is one part of the story. But, on the other hand, Teilhard holds strongly that the believer has been partly responsible for the growth of contemporary unbelief by his reluctance to recognize the profound significance and value of the natural world. It is, of course, true that the Church has no special competence in the field of material, physical, biological and historical happenings. It is also true that, at times, it is necessary for the believer to withdraw from 'the world'. Renunciation is undoubtedly a necessary element in that process of self-discipline which fallen man requires in order to achieve harmony and balance.

But this renunciation is not an end in itself; it is not, or should not be, an abiding attitude of mind, except in the case of the small minority of Christians who may have a special vocation within the total body. In a letter he remarks:

I am beginning to think that there is a certain aspect of

14. 'Mastery of the World and the Kingdom of God', *Writings in Time of War*, p. 85.

the real world as closed to some believers as the world of faith is to unbelievers.[15]

The aspect is, of course, the theological truth that God is present to and active in his creation, no less effectively and far more profoundly and immediately than ever was painter in the growth of his landscape or sculptor in the emergence of the statue. The Christian who turns away from, 'despises', the things of the earth is much worse than the so-called music-lover who is so interested in the life and character of Beethoven that he cannot be bothered to listen to a performance of a Beethoven symphony.

He is in a worse case. For Beethoven has completed his work. All that musicians can do is to play his compositions over and over again, adding nuances of interpretation, perhaps, trying to recapture the mind and purpose of the man who wrote the original score. But, since the world is still in process of development, moving towards its final consummation; since the creator is no remote clock-maker who, having wound up the cosmic mechanism, allows it to run its course in some predetermined fashion; since, on the contrary, both the revealed Word of God and the very history of man bear witness to the obvious fact that the creator has vested in his creature man dominion over all living things and over all the resources of the earth; since, in a word, man is created in the very image of God, part of his duty is to co-operate with his creator in bringing the universe to its final goal.

The ordinary Christian, then, must learn to realize that the world-process is something in which he is, not merely passively but most actively, involved. The on-

15. *Letters from a Traveller*, p. 66; Fontana, p. 28.

ward movement of mankind to an ever richer and more splendid fulfilment necessarily demands the full collaboration of man himself. His intellectual powers, his developing skills, his sensitivity, all, in short, that makes him a human being, is to be put at the disposal of his master, not by some thwarting or renunciation of them but by the most intense and passionate application of them to the sheer demands of human living. In the words which Teilhard must have heard and read a thousand times in the course of his life as a schoolboy and as a Jesuit,

Man has been created to praise, reverence and serve God, and in this way to save his soul.

In what might almost be a gloss on this sentence, he asks:

Who then, at last, will be the *ideal Christian*, the Christian, at once new and old, who will solve in his soul the problem of this vital balance, by allowing all the life-sap of the world to pass into his effort towards the divine Trinity?[16]

The way in which he will do this will vary with his individual capacities and opportunities. Yet there is one duty incumbent on all Christians as it is incumbent on all men everywhere. This is the duty—though that is too cold a word—to love. For love is the fundamental impulse of life or, to put it in his own preferred language, 'the one natural medium in which the rising course of evolution can proceed'. Omit love, and we are faced with the prospect (already to some extent realized, not only in the totalitarian systems of our day but in the soulless techniques of any large-scale technological society) of standardization and enslavement. It is through

16. 'Mastery of the World and the Kingdom of God', op. cit., p. 88.

love that we must look for the deepening of our most intimate selves, in the life-giving coming together of mankind. Love is the free and imaginative outpouring of spirit. It links those who love in bonds that unite but do not confound.

There is a striking parallel to this idea in the words of a ninth-century theologian:

It is the nature of lower things to be drawn to and absorbed in the higher, not in such a way that they cease to be, but so that they are more fully preserved in the higher, and they subsist, and are one.[17]

In the familiar words of St John, 'God is love: everyone who loves is a child of God and knows God, but the unloving know nothing of God'. Teilhard would comment on this that as we discover God in all the works of his creation, it is most specifically in the experience of love that we know him most truly. Moreover, he would urge us to develop in our lives a truly creative love, until, in his words, God becomes finally all in all, in an atmosphere of sheer love.

This sounds like and could be taken to be nothing more than a rather conventional peroration to a pious exhortation, sending its hearers away with a nice comfortable warm glow inside them, but without any very clear idea as to what precisely it means in practice. Teilhard had no sort of doubt. For him the love of God meant the love of God's world; and the love of God's world meant the energetic working for its perfection, since this is man's whole purpose. Nothing could be higher or nobler than to collaborate with God

17. Quoted in Henri de Lubac, *The Religion of Teilhard de Chardin* (Collins, London, and Desclée, New York, 1967), p. 152.

in promoting God's plan. What that plan is can best be seen -by looking at the world of God's making, seeing how it works, what has gone to its formation, how best its resources can be developed.

How this must influence all our conduct we shall be considering more at length in a later section. For the present it is necessary to insist on the fact that Teilhard did not dissolve away all the traditional elements of Christian practice, whether in direct worship of God, in ascetic training, or in personal devotion and the like, in order to substitute a vague religion of mere activity in the service of our fellow-men. He would agree, of course, that the most concrete and specific test of our religious faith is the measure of our involvement in the affairs of our fellow-men. 'Anyone who says "I love God" and hates his brother is a liar, since a man who does not love the brother that he can see cannot love God, whom he has never seen' (1 John 4:20). He would agree with von Hügel:

> . . . only a vivid faith in the utterly real and perfect God, only the experience and love of eternal life, are able, in the long run, to supply a sufficiently deep, steady, and tender love and service of our fellow-creatures, precisely where, in their actual condition, they most require, because they least deserve, such selfless devotion.[18]

It is central to his teaching that we can come to know God only through his creation. But it is not less but more important to recognize that he held that we did come to *God* and not just to God-in-the-world. As he said,

18. *Eternal Life* (T. & T. Clark, Edinburgh, 1912), p. 316.

> There is a communion with God and a communion
> with earth, and a communion with God through
> the earth.[19]

Communion with earth and communion with God
through earth are indeed important aspects of our
human and Christian responsibilities. But to suggest
that they exhaust those responsibilities is, he would
hold, completely to misunderstand the essential situation.
God is, at once, transcendent and imminent. He

> cannot in any way be intermixed with or lost in the
> participated being which he sustains and animates and
> holds together, but he is at the birth and the growth
> and the final term of all things.[20]

For Teilhard, it is the human personality, the spiritual
reality that man is, that is the high point of evolution.

> Everything becomes, if not spirit, at least a distant
> preparation for, 'matter' for, spirit.[21]

> The world is . . . *fundamentally* and *initially* living,
> and its whole history is basically just one vast psychic
> operation: the slow but progressive concentration of
> a diffuse consciousness.[22]

> Spirit is not something superimposed on or a by-
> product of the cosmos, but represents simply the
> higher state assumed in us . . .[23]

Therefore it follows that the reality that underlies and
controls this onward movement must be at least personal.
Hence,

> The deeper I descend into myself the more I find God
> at the heart of my being,[24]

and indeed

19. C. Cuénot, op. cit., p. 38.
20. 'Cosmic Life', *Writings in Time of War*, p. 47.
21. E. Rideau, op. cit., p. 81.   22. Ibid.   23. Ibid.
24. 'Cosmic Life', op. cit., p. 61.

the supremely personal God, from whom we are the
more distinct, the more we lose ourselves in him.[25]

Yet such a 'loss' of self in God does not mean a merging
of the personal selfhood with a kind of spiritual
Moloch devouring his children. Not for Teilhard is
Rupert Brooke's gospel—'A pulse in the eternal mind'.
Rather, the origin and term of the whole cosmic process
is

> a living, loving Being, in which the individual con-
> sciousness, when it is lost, attains an accentuation and
> an illumination that extends to the furthest limits of
> what is contained in its own personality. . . . No
> words can express the bliss of feeling oneself pos-
> sessed, absorbed, without end or limit, by an Infinite
> that is not rarefied and colourless, but living and
> luminous, an Infinite that knows and attracts and
> loves.[26]

Whatever the scientific bent of his mind, whatever the
absorption in his research and exploration, whatever his
passionate concern for his fellow-men, we can hardly
doubt the sincerity of the ringing cry,

> I am exclusively and madly in love with the divine
> influence that guides the world.[27]

Yet it would be wrong to conclude from this sort of
language, or from the many passages in his published
works in which he preaches the presence of God in the
world, that he himself knew nothing of those uncer-
tainties and questionings which are the experience of
most believers. As he had said himself in 1916,

25. H. de Lubac, *The Faith of Teilhard de Chardin*, p. 16.
26. 'Cosmic Life', op. cit., p. 48.
27. Letter of 31 July 1930.

The realities of faith are not felt with the same solidity as the reality of experience . . .[28]

In the notes which he left of his various annual retreats, we learn how much he had to struggle to make God 'real again in life'.

The true Foundation is not a logical relationship . . . that relationship is evident . . . What we lack is the sense of the reality of God, it is complete faith . . . Really to believe that you exist, my God. That's where the whole difficulty lies—for everyone, I imagine. . . . Maybe it is inevitable, maybe it is well, and necessary, that I should feel at every moment as though I can advance no further, never sure of the next step.[29]

Anyone who has seriously tried to lead a spiritual life will see in Teilhard a colleague and a fellow-pilgrim. Intellectually he may seem a giant among pigmies. When it comes to the practice of seeking God in Himself, even through His creation, he emerges as beset with the same doubts and problems and anxieties, the same sense of personal inadequacy which is the necessary condition of a relationship between creature and Creator.

One last quotation, from one of his early letters, may serve to sum up this stage of Teilhard's spiritual doctrine. He writes that he is now 'more sharply aware that for the rest of my life my task is to develop in myself, humbly, faithfully, doggedly—and at the same time to impart it as much as possible to others—the sort of mysticism that makes one seek passionately for God in the heart of every substance and every action. Never have I so clearly seen how God alone, and no personal

28. *The Making of a Mind*, p. 145.
29. H. de Lubac, *The Faith of Teilhard de Chardin*, pp. 82-3.

effort, can open our eyes to this light and preserve this vision in us. And never, on the other hand, have I understood so fully how much the practice of this particular science of divinizing life calls for the diligent co-operation of every form of activity I engage in. It needs the sacraments, and prayer . . . and study: all these directed to the same concrete, very precise, end.'[30]

'It needs the sacraments and prayer and study.' If the goal of his efforts was expressed at times in a novel form, the means remained as traditional as they could be.

2

CHRIST

I want to love Christ with all my strength in the very act of loving the universe. Can this be absurdity, blasphemy?[1]

The universal Christ, as I understood the name, is a synthesis of Christ and the universe. He is not a new godhead—but an inevitable deployment of the mystery in which Christianity is summed up, the mystery of the Incarnation.[2]

Christ is loved as a person; he compels recognition as a world.[3]

30. *The Making of a Mind*, pp. 190-1.

1. Letter of 15 March 1916.
2. *How I Believe* (Collins, London, 1969), p. 37.
3. 'The Priest', *Writings in Time of War*, p. 213.

New Testament criticism, outside Roman Catholic circles, was dominated during most of the nineteenth century by the so-called search for the historical Jesus, the human being whose life and teaching had been obscured, distorted or simply falsified by the early Church which had constructed the Christ of faith, embodying ideas and theological conceptions which were never uttered or even conceived by Jesus of Nazareth. Although at the time when Teilhard was studying theology at Ore Place, such ideas were anathema in official Roman Catholic circles, and there is no evidence that he was ever especially interested in scriptural studies as such, he would doubtless have regarded the whole topic as a somewhat arid academic exercise. Of course it is true that we cannot now recapture the precise lineaments of the character and appearance, the tone of voice and the actual language of the Son of man. We cannot be sure that his earliest disciples understood him aright, or even remembered exactly what he had said. Of course their vision of him, as they looked back over the years, across the events of the last days of his earthly sojourn, might well have taken on a certain quality, almost a new dimension, of significance which had never been present to their minds as they actually listened to him.

The only thing that mattered was that this earthly life of the man Jesus had started a whole train of ever richer and more fruitful developments in man's outlook on the world, which has shown itself able to take in and accommodate whatever fresh discoveries might be made in whatever field of human endeavour. The failure of Christians in their religious faith was their reluctance to recognize that they were committed, by the very fact of the Incarnation, to what we may call a bi-focal view of history. On the one hand, it was essential to hold on to the reality of Christ's sheer humanity.

> The more I reflect upon the profound laws of evolution, the more I am convinced that the universal Christ would be unable to appear at the end of time at the world summit unless he had previously been inserted into the course of the world's movement *by way of birth* in the form of an element. If it is really by Christ-Omega that the world is held in movement, then, for our own experience, it is from his concrete source, the man of Nazareth, that Christ-Omega draws (theoretically and historically) his whole stability.[4]

On the other hand, the 'Christ of faith' is so much more than the 'Jesus of history', simply because, in virtue of the divine nature operative in and through the purely human qualities of mind and body which grew together in stature during those thirty-odd years from Bethlehem to Calvary, the achievement of the son of Mary is something that is at least conterminous with the whole range of created history, in space as well as in time. It does, of course, outsoar those confines even whilst it totally interpenetrates whatever exists within them.

> Concretely and historically it is incontestable that the living and conquering idea of the universal Christ appeared and developed in the Christian consciousness when Jesus the man was adored and recognized as God.[5]

4. *Christianisme et évolution*, 1945 (unpublished).
5. Quoted in Christopher F. Mooney, *Teilhard de Chardin and the Mystery of Christ* (Collins, London, 1966), p. 73.

Yet, alas,

> In spite of the repeated assertions of St Paul and the Greek Fathers, Christ's universal power over creation has hitherto been considered by theologians primarily in an extrinsic and juridical aspect. 'Christ is King of the world, because his Father *declared* him to be King' . . . . Except in regard to the mysterious 'sanctifying grace', the organic side of the Incarnation, and in consequence its physical presuppositions or conditions, were relegated to the background: the more readily so, in that the recent and terrifying increased dimensions of our universe (in volume, duration, and number) seemed finally to make physical control of the cosmic totality by the Person Christ, inconceivable.[6]

Teilhard's views are strongly supported by that great Augustinian scholar, Professor H. I. Marrou :

> The historian knows . . . to what an extent the feeling for the cosmic scope of Christian salvation has been progressively blurred and atrophied in Western theology. This we must blame (and I am in a good position to know this) on the influence of St Augustine, whose psychological depth and richness are given full play to the detriment of his interest in the world.
>
> And, paradoxically, this atrophy became more pronounced at the very time when the development of modern civilization was turning more and more on knowing and mastering the forces of nature. From this arose the ever-widening gap between modern civilization and the Christian message; the latter seemed to dissociate itself from the former, to have nothing to say

6. *Science and Christ* (Collins, London, and Harper & Row, New York, 1968), pp. 165-6.

to it and nothing to contribute to it, when, in fact, our civilization has a most urgent need to be animated, taken in hand, exorcized, baptized, confirmed.[7]

It was to the task of enabling men to see what he passionately believed to be the true Christology, the authentic appreciation of the function of the total Christ, that Teilhard early dedicated himself.

The various regions, nations, social groupings, have each their particular apostles.

And I, Lord, for my (very lowly) part, would wish to be the apostle—and if I dare be so bold, the evangelist—*of your Christ in the universe*.[8]

This meant, in effect, that, whilst accepting and appreciating all the traditional pieties and devotions that centred themselves on the humanity of Christ, he would insist that these must not be thought of 'out of context', dissociated from that larger and fuller vision of Christ 'ever greater', growing in man's understanding of him as man's knowledge of the universe grew and expanded. It meant, not least, the end of any purely individualistic and self-regarding cultivation of the Christian virtues.

'The sovereign charm of Christianity', according to Teilhard, 'is that it is above all a religion of persons, the religion of souls . . . the Christian believes that he holds within himself an immortal substance, an incorruptible fruit which is the object of every process and every proliferation in the universe. . . . in each one of the souls that is born from it, and then takes flight, the cosmos is incessantly fulfilling its finest hopes.'[9] Yet this

7. *Témoignage chrétien*, 22 April 1955.
8. 'The Priest', op. cit., p. 219.
9. 'Cosmic Life', *Writings in Time of War*, p. 46.

does not mean and must not be taken to mean that
Christianity is concerned merely with the sanctification
of the individual. Apart altogether from the fact that, as
we know, human beings can achieve their fulfilment as
human beings only in communion with others—in the
family, the social group, the larger political organization
—one of the important doctrines of Christian theology is
that of the mystical body of Christ. This was, to Teilhard, an immensely precious and inspiring truth. For
he saw it as enshrining, in all its developing variety, the
importance of human beings, simply as human beings,
the appeal of Christ himself as the perfect man, with all
that meant of moral integrity, human sympathy and
understanding love, spiritual excellence at all levels, joy
in human achievement and in the works of God's
hands, the powerful example of courage in suffering and
its lesson of redemptive achievement. Above all he
welcomed the doctrine because it showed how revelation
comes in to underwrite and authenticate all the lessons
he had sought to teach others out of his personal
experience.

Yet it must always be borne in mind that he never
lost sight of the double polarity of his faith; that it is a
supremely individualist religion and, at the same time, essentially a cosmic one. We can begin to understand what
this means by looking first at his own personal relationship to Christ. We recall first how he had learnt from
his mother that devotion to the Sacred Heart of
Jesus which was to abide with him throughout his life.
Thus, in a letter written from the Front in 1916, he
says,

From the practical point of view I am glad that

tomorrow happens to be the feast of the Sacred Heart. The master above all of the interior life.[10]

And, less than a year later, he writes again,

Among the things Blessed Margaret Mary relates, there's one that has always struck me particularly: I mean the vision in which she seemed to be an indeterminate atom striving to lose herself in the great centre of light that was the heart of our Lord, and unable to do so until the centre itself drew her in ... In this account I recognize the two elements which sum up life for me: *absolute dependence* on the creative and sanctifying energy of God, which alone can maintain rooted in us the passion for life, the passion for God; and then, once this deep-seated attraction has been implanted in us, *an invasion by the divinity* of our whole achievement, of all we do, so that for us everything becomes the self-giving, transforming God.[11]

It is then hardly surprising that in 1923 he is meditating as follows:

How strange, my God, are the processes your spirit initiates: When, two centuries ago, your Church began to feel the particular power of your heart, it might have seemed that what was captivating men's souls was the fact of their finding in you an element even more determinate, more circumscribed, than your humanity as a whole. But now on the contrary a swift reversal is making us aware that your main purpose in this revealing to us of your heart was to enable our love to escape from the constrictions of the too narrow, too precise, too limited image of you which we had fashioned for ourselves. What I

10. *The Making of a Mind*, p. 107.   11. Ibid., p. 192.

discern in your breast is simply a furnace of fire; and
the more I fix my gaze on its ardency the more it
seems to me that all around it the contours of your
body melt away and become enlarged beyond all
measure, till the only features I can distinguish in
you are those of the face of a world which has burst
into flame.[12]

But it is important that we should not interpret this
and similar passages in terms of a vague mystagogy. As
a scientist Teilhard naturally started from the facts
given in the investigation of some individual concrete
situation, even though his speculations soared far beyond that particular event. So it is with his religious
thought.

If you suppress the historical reality of Christ, the
divine omnipresence which intoxicates us becomes
. . . uncertain, vague . . . lacking the decisive experimental verification by which to impose itself on
our minds, and without the moral authority to assimilate our lives into it. Thenceforward, however
dazzling the expansions which we shall try in a
moment to discern in the resurrected Christ, their
beauty and their stuff of reality will always remain
inseparable from the tangible and verifiable truth of
the Gospel event. The mystical Christ, the universal
Christ of St Paul, has neither meaning nor value in
our eyes except as an expansion of the Christ who was
born of Mary and who died on the cross. . . . However far we may be drawn into the divine spaces
opened up to us by Christian mysticism, we never
depart from the Jesus of the Gospels.[13]

12. *Hymn of the Universe*, p. 34; Fontana, p. 32.
13. *Le Milieu Divin*, p. 105; Fontana, p. 117; U.S. ed., pp. 94-5.

At the same time, he was well aware of the danger of seeing the full Christian message exclusively in terms of its undeveloped, undeveloping form as it was first delivered to the followers of Christ. The danger was twofold. On the one hand, such an attitude was liable to stunt the growth of the believer, whose eyes might be ever turning back to the 'simple world' of the first century in a form of escapism from the demands of life in the twentieth century. It was to such men that Christ's own words were addressed. 'None of you asks me: Where are you going? Yet you are plunged in grief because of what I have just said. Nevertheless I tell you the truth: it is for your own good that I am leaving you. You see, if I don't go the Counsellor won't come to you: if I go, I will send him to you . . . There is still much that I could say to you, but the burden is beyond your present strength. However, when he comes who is the Spirit of truth, he will lead you forward into the fullness of truth . . . and he will make known to you the things that lie in the future . . . All that the Father has is mine and that is why I have just said: Everything that he makes known to you he will draw from what belongs to me.' In other words, Our Lord himself invites his followers to look beyond that temporal situation in which he became incarnate, and in which his life as an individual man was led. To think exclusively in terms of his localized experience is to belittle and impoverish the totality of his teaching—a teaching to be progressively unfolded and appreciated under the influence of his Spirit.

It is precisely because Christianity has too often been presented exclusively in such terms that the other danger has arisen—a threat to faith in face of the colossal changes that have come over the world-picture since the days of Christ.

The enrichment and ferment of religious thought in our time has undoubtedly been caused by the revelation of the size and the unity of the world all around us and within us . . .

To some, the world has disclosed itself as too vast; within such immensity, man is lost and no longer counts; and there is nothing left for him to do but shut his eyes and disappear. To others, on the contrary, the world is too beautiful; and it, and it alone, must be adored.

There are Christians who . . . are alarmed by the agitation or the attraction invincibly produced in them by this new rising star. Is the Christ of the Gospels, imagined and loved within the dimensions of a Mediterranean world, capable of still embracing and still forming the centre of our prodigiously expanded universe? Is the world not in the process of becoming more vast, more close, more dazzling than Jehovah? Will it not burst our religion asunder? Eclipse our God?[14]

For Teilhard the answer was given nineteen hundred years ago by St Paul, in the generation after the Resurrection of Christ. Speaking of Christ, he has this to say: 'He is the image of the invisible God; his is the primacy over all created things. In him everything in heaven and on earth was created . . . the whole universe has been created through him and for him. He is at the head and front of all things; in him all things are bound together. He is also the head of the body, the

14. *Le Milieu Divin*, pp. 13-14; Fontana, pp. 45-6; U.S. ed., pp. 13-14.

Church; its origin, as first-born of the dead. You see he was to be supreme in all things. For God chose to establish in him the fullness of all that exists. Through him God chose to reconcile the whole of reality in him . . . reconciling through him alone everything that is on earth or in heaven.'

In other words, Christianity, from its very beginnings, has accepted the notion that, in some unfathomable way, in the being of him who appeared on earth as the man Jesus of Nazareth, the whole explanation, the whole purpose of the vast fabric of creation, from its material origins to the highest manifestations of spirit, is to be found. The answer to the riddle of the universe is: Christ Jesus.

But if this answer is to satisfy modern man, it will be necessary to enlarge its scope to contain all the values that modern man has come to accept.

The expression of our Christology is still exactly the same as that which, three centuries ago, was sufficient for men . . . the four-thousand-year-old world . . . for which our theological textbooks were written.[15]
But for modern man, this sort of cosmic picture has become insupportable. Moreover, apart from this inadequate cosmology, the presentation of Christ has been too extrinsic and individualistic. Christ is not presented as he should be, in terms of his cosmic function, as indicated by St Paul. Men have been given a picture of Christ, dissociated from the universe, a detached fragment bringing men into conflict with one another.

'How then', Teilhard goes on to ask, 'may we conceive Christ to be constituted as the cosmic centre of creation?

15. *Christologie et évolution*, 1933 (unpublished).

Simply as a magnification, a transformation, realized in the humanity of Christ, of the *aura* that surrounds every human monad.'[16]

In the case of other human beings, we have experience, from time to time, of leaders who are at once centres of attraction and points at which some corporate activity concentrates and develops. We can think of great political figures such as Abraham Lincoln or Winston Churchill; we can think of great artists such as Michelangelo, Shakespeare or Beethoven; we can think of the great inventors and scientific thinkers—Copernicus, Lister, Marconi and Rutherford . . . All these men have given a fresh impulse to the human spirit, by providing centres of psychic energy, round which the efforts of countless individuals have collected and found inspiration. Analogously we can think of Christ, the man, the son of Mary, chosen so that his influence, his *aura*, might serve as the medium in which men's united efforts could be enlarged and given a fresh direction, dominating and drawing them all to himself. Such influence is to be seen as possessing a basis both natural and supernatural. The very doctrine of the Incarnation means that the supernatural being of God has assumed a natural form in order to enter our universe. This in turn implies that Christ both inspires and claims for himself the natural desires of man's heart. For, as Teilhard argues, 'If the *supernatural* term of the world did not at the same time "round it off" naturally, it would leave the universe facing a void, and our hearts impervious to feeling.'[17] 'There is only *one single centre* in the universe; it is at once

16. 'Forma Christi', Writings in Time of War, p. 253.
17. Ibid., p. 255, note 6.

natural and supernatural; it impels the whole of creation along one and the same line, first towards the fullest development of consciousness, and later towards the highest degree of holiness: in other words towards Christ Jesus, personal and cosmic.'[18]

Teilhard wrestles again and again with this difficult concept of a 'cosmic' Christ, in order to give it greater significance and spiritual effectiveness. He returns to the idea of human individuality as we normally think of it. We have got used to thinking of human beings as so many separate units, independent of each other, isolated from other individuals and from the universe itself. At the level of ordinary social contacts this may well be true. Yet no man can achieve his full personality, develop his talents, become 'himself' in isolation. He needs the interplay of other minds, he is even supported in his physical existence by a whole fabric of natural elements and forces. He needs air, food, clothing and other *things* which can come into being only because of the complicated network of nature in its rich variety. If the universe is constituted of its myriad elements, the elements in turn need the universe for their existence. So we must say of every man that, over and above his body and soul, there is a physical relationship binding him to the universe in which he finds his fulfilment. And, just as he himself is in a continuous process of development, of becoming himself, so is the whole cosmos a growing and developing whole. Just as the cells combine to make a human body so do human beings themselves combine to make up that total, but as yet unrealized, fulfilment which is the cosmos-to-be.

So is it with Christ. In his human nature, he is this

18. Ibid., p. 256.

individual, born of Mary, nurtured in Bethlehem and Nazareth, 'advancing in wisdom' as he learnt from his mother, his teachers, his friends. He too needed the support of nature's resources, as he needed the support of friendship and love. At that level he is an element in the cosmos. But we know, from St John and St Paul, that he is also the centre of creation, the force which can subject all things to itself, the origin and the term of the whole cosmic process—Alpha and Omega. Hence, just as we have seen that there is a certain physical relationship which both perfects him and enables him to contribute to the perfection of the universe, so there is a relationship of all beings, but, in a special sense, of the members of his body to Christ. Just as there is something of the cosmos in each individual constituent of it, so there is something of Christ in every creature. It is the responsibility as it is the privilege of each to develop that Christ-element within himself, thus adding to the fullness that Christ, in himself, already is.

We are familiar with the passage in which St Paul tells the Colossians: 'It is now my happiness to suffer for you. This is my way of helping to complete, in my poor human flesh, the full tale of Christ's sufferings still to be endured, for the sake of his body.' Teilhard would extend this idea to all our human activities, whereby we help to complete the full tale of Christ's achievement. 'For it is in Christ that the complete being of God dwells in corporeal form and it is in him that you have been brought to your perfection.' But this perfection is no solitary achievement, any more than it is a solitary effort. It is a corporate achievement as it is a corporate effort. 'He is the head and on him the whole body depends. Bonded and knit together by every constituent joint, the whole frame grows through the due activity of every part and builds up in love.' So St Paul speaks, writing to the church of Ephesus. And Teilhard develops without falsifying the thought:

God, who is as immense and all-embracing as matter, and at the same time as warm and intimate as a soul, is the centre who spreads through all things . . . Souls are irresistibly drawn by the demands of their innate powers, and still more by the call of grace, towards a common centre of beatitude, and it is in this convergence that they find a first bond that combines them in a natural whole. . . .

Moreover, grace, which introduces them into the field of divine attraction, forces them all to exert an influence, as they proceed, upon one another; and it is in this relation of dependence . . . that there lies so astonishingly 'cosmic' mystery of the *Communion of Saints*.

Like particles immersed in one and the same spiritual field, souls cannot think or pray or act or move, without waves being produced . . . which set the others in motion. . . .

Grace, in fact, is more than the common environment or over-all current by which the multitude is bound together into one solid whole, one single impulse. The Communion of Saints is held together in the hallowed unity of a physically organized whole; and this whole—more absolute than the individuals over which it has dominion, in as much as the elements penetrate into and subsist in God, as a *function* of him and *not as isolated particles*—this whole is the body of Christ.[19]

19. 'Cosmic Life', op. cit., p. 48.

Christ organizes himself for us and implants himself in us. But he demands the co-operation of our good will and our actions. This necessary co-operation we give him by exerting ourselves to become assimilated, by lovingly submitting our own independence to his. This assimilation lies in loving kindness and humility, in community, in community of suffering by which the Passion of Calvary is continued and completed; but above all in charity, that wonderful virtue which makes us see and cherish Christ in every man and so enables us to promote, in the immediacy of a single act, the unification of all in one. This is the body of Christ, which seeks to be realized in each one of us.

The very breadth and universality of Teilhard's vision was such that there is some danger of our failing to realize how greatly he was, at the same time, concerned with the individual, and the perfection of the individual. This concern is well brought out in an essay he wrote during his stay in China where, as we have seen, he spent the whole of the Second World War. The title of the essay is 'Super-Humanity, Super-Christ, Super-Charity'[20]—a Teilhardian conception if ever there was one. A close study of what he writes here will serve as an admirable illustration both of the way in which he related his scientific convictions to his Christian faith and also of his ability to see the wood and the trees in one clear perspective. The mere term 'super-humanity' might suggest a sort of Nietzschean fantasy of a race of supermen. But this is far from the truth as Teilhard saw it. Beginning with the sentence, highly relevant to our general theme, that 'Intellectually, morally and mystically we are no longer satisfied with what was

20. *Science and Christ*, pp. 151 ff.

good enough for our fathers,'[21] he goes on to argue that the facts make it clear that a new humanity is in process of development. The history of man's evolution shows an increasing intensity both of intellectual power and of what he calls 'socialization', so much so that the two seem to be linked by some sort of intrinsic connection. As man becomes more intelligent, so does he tend towards a closer association with his fellows. It is true that there are groupings of animate beings which are marked by a strong 'sense' of community—the ant-hill, the beehive—but at the subhuman level animate units behave chiefly as 'links or gears'. They 'transmit rather than exist'.

When we come to man, we find a new characteristic emerging. Precisely because man can reflect upon himself, can turn inwards, there is about him a unique quality. He is a 'centre of incommunicable value, a value that cannot be transmitted'. Man is, in Kant's phrase, 'an end and not a mere means'. Yet this must not be understood to mean, 'as some scientifically and morally disastrous theories hold', that evolution has reached its final term in man, that 'the human being is released from every nexus and further development in the . . . collective plane'. As we have already seen, Teilhard along with other contemporary scientists such as Sir Julian Huxley, holds that the onward march of evolution can and must be controlled and assisted by man's intelligent activity.

But what this view of man's uniqueness does involve is this important consequence, namely that man cannot enter into any complexity of a higher order unless this has the effect of preserving and even increasing that

21. Ibid., p. 151.

specific characteristic which he alone possesses, the characteristic of personality. The growing collectivization which, as he argues, goes hand in hand with man's growing intelligence—which should, therefore, be the next stage in the story of man's progress—can only mean a heightening of his personality. But, 'since only the forces of love have the property of personalizing by uniting', this means that man must grow in sympathy and unanimity.

> It is in the direction and in the form of a single heart that we must look for our picture of super-mankind, rather even than in that of a single brain.[22]

Once again, we see Teilhard 'extrapolating' (to use one of his favourite words) from the purely scientific analysis to the religious and spiritual. The scientist would doubtless question the rigour of his demonstration. To the believer there is something quite fascinating about the transition from the sphere of the technical to the realm of the ascetic and mystical. To the Christian two utterances of Our Lord spring to mind: 'He that loses his life for my sake shall find it.' By going out of yourself, losing yourself in another, you find yourself, you become more of a person, more yourself. And again: 'By this will all men know that you are my disciples, if you have love one for another.'

Moreover, by thus growing in personal stature, we help on the growth of the body of Christ, we bring about a Super-Christ.

> By Super-Christ I most certainly do not mean *another* Christ, a second Christ different from and greater than the first. I mean *the same* Christ, the Christ of all time, revealing himself to us in a form and in

22. Ibid., p. 160.

dimensions, with an urgency and area of contact, that are enlarged and given a new force. . . . Both in nature and in function Christ gathers up in himself and consummates the totality and the fullness of humanity.[23]

Returning to the previous stage of his argument, he goes on:

If . . . the evidence obliges our reason to accept that something greater than the man of today is in gestation upon earth, it means that in order to be able to continue to worship as before we must be able to say to ourselves, as we look at the Son of man [not '*Apparuit humanitas*', but] '*Apparuit Superhumanitas*'.[24]

Here Teilhard plunges boldly into theology, taking issue with the traditionalists who, neglecting the teaching of St Paul and the Greek Fathers, have disregarded what he calls the 'organic' side of the Incarnation. The role of Christ in creation has been restricted to the purely spiritual and supernatural, the redemption of the world through the operation of sanctifying grace. The reluctance of theologians to consider the purely physical relationship existing between the incarnate Word and the material creation has been intensified by the discoveries of modern science.

. . . the recent and terrifying increased dimensions of our universe (in volume, duration, and number) seemed finally to make physical control of the cosmic totality by the Person Christ, inconceivable.[25]

This, of course, represented not merely a failure of imagination, which is more pardonable in a theologian, but a failure of faith, faith precisely in the fact that in

23. Ibid., p. 164.   24. Ibid.   25. Ibid., p. 166.

Christ we have to do not with a human person but with a human nature which is the concrete manifestation and expression of a divinely personal nature. Imperturbably, Teilhard sweeps on:

> . . . St Paul's boldest sayings readily take on a literal meaning as soon as the world is seen to be suspended, by its conscious side, from an Omega Point of convergence, and Christ, in virtue of his Incarnation, is recognized as carrying out precisely the functions of Omega.[26]

And not merely St Paul. Teilhard might well have invoked here the stupendous opening of the Fourth Gospel.

> In the beginning was the Word . . . and the Word was God . . . Through him all things came to be, not one thing had its being but through him. All that came to be had life in him . . .

The eternal Logos, the Idea in the Divine Mind, expressing not merely the full truth about the Godhead itself but also the truth about all the activity of God *ad extra*, beyond himself, in the work of creation. Nothing, therefore, that exists or can exist could possibly fall outside the ambit of that all-embracing Idea. The vaster becomes our knowledge of the universe, the more will our minds be stretched to appreciate the grandeur of the Word—'the Christ of all time revealing himself to us in a form and in dimensions, with an urgency and area of contact that are enlarged and given a new force.'

For it is this very Word that becomes flesh, is somehow incorporated in, involved with, the very process of evolution which, at the same time, he controls. But that control, at the natural, practical level, is exercised through the agency of his fellow-men. The more com-

26. Ibid.

plete and adequate that control, the more clearly will
the Idea, the Word, the origin and final purpose of the
universe be appreciated, understood, accepted and loved.
To put it in the form of more popular devotional
Christianity, if it is true that we must look for our
picture of super-mankind in the form of a single heart,
that heart will turn out to be the heart of Christ.
Mystical? Unrealistic? Out of the world? Hardly, if we
continue with Teilhard's argument.

To say that Christ is the term and motive force of evolution, to say that he manifests himself as 'evolver', is
implicitly to recognize that he becomes attainable in
and through the whole process of evolution. Let us
examine the consequences for our interior life of this
amazing situation.

There are three, and they may be expressed as
follows: 'Under the influence of the Super-Christ, our
charity is universalized, becomes dynamic and is
synthesized.'[27]

There is little need to dwell on the first two of the
three requirements. That Christian love ought to be
universal is one of the platitudes of the preacher. Yet
it may be not irrelevant to point out that, in accordance
with Teilhard's own views, the very advances in the
techniques of mass media, the rapidity of communica-
tions and the constant demand for information met by a
growing sophistication of journalistic enterprise, have
compelled us to enlarge our horizons to take in the
sufferings of remote populations, the problems of coun-
tries far distant from our own, the feats of human
endurance and skill which are all presented to us, as
they happen, on our television screens and radio trans-

27. Ibid., p. 167.

mitters. The very scale of the demands made upon our emotions and our sympathy may blunt our sensibilities unless these are heightened and sharpened by an increasing spiritualization of outlook, enabling us to see that,

> As the mystics felt instinctively, everything becomes physically and literally lovable in God; and God, in return, becomes intelligible and lovable in everything around us.[28]

And, whilst there will literally be no limit to the range of demands on our love, so there will be no slackening in its intensity. The 'dynamic' charity that Teilhard demands is not the traditional attitude of contemplation and compassion, the contemplation of God that seeks 'to rise above human distractions and passions in order to find rest in the light and unvarying warmth of the divine Sun'; the compassion which contented itself with binding up the wounds of a stricken humanity, but felt no need to fulfil a more positive role. But now,

> To co-operate in total cosmic evolution is the only deliberate act that can adequately express our devotion to an evolutive and universal Christ.[29]

What, then, is meant by the term 'synthesized'? In the context it is used as an antithesis to the condition whereby all too often, 'our interior life remains fragmented and pluralized'. This is because in our relationships with impersonal beings and even in our human inter-relationships we encounter these objects only 'tangentially'—not because of who or what they are in themselves, but simply because of some interest, some business matter which brings us into association with them. What we need to develop is a relationship with them *in terms of Christ*, a Christ loved in and

28. Ibid., p. 168.   29. Ibid., p. 169.

for himself but also as the heart of the multitude, the plurality of his universe. If he gives to all his creatures their meaning and their value, then, by loving him in them, we are at the same time loving them for what they are, because they are what he has made them.

Eating, drinking, working, seeking; creating truth or beauty or happiness; all these things could, until now, has seemed to us heterogeneous, disparate activities, incapable of being reduced to terms of one another—loving being no more than one of a number of branches in this divergent physical efflorescence.

Now, however, that it is directed towards the Super-Christ, the fascicle draws itself together . . .

Originally, the Christian had no desire except to be able to love, at all times and whatever he was doing, *at the same time as he was acting*. Now he sees that he can love *by his activity*, in other words he can directly be united to the divine centre by his every action, no matter what form it may take.[30]

In so far as Teilhard is talking of our relationship with our fellow human beings, what he is saying is, in effect, no more than the age-old summons of Christ himself. 'As long as you did it to the least of these my little ones you did it to me.' Where he goes beyond this teaching, he is perhaps as he would say 'extrapolating', though he might well claim that he is only trying to make a little more specific the implications of the Lord's Prayer: 'Thy kingdom come . . . on earth as in heaven.' Teilhard's idea of the perfection of the Christian man might still be expressed in the traditional phrase: the following of Christ. But this has all too often been interpreted as meaning little more than the

30. Ibid. pp. 170-1.

attempt to reproduce in our own lives the specific features of Christ's earthly experience, as though the accidental shape imposed on him by a particular historical and sociological situation possessed in itself ,some transcendental value. The Christ we are called upon to follow is the Christ who is the head and front of the evolutionary process, not the Galilean preacher *as such*, not even the victim of Jewish envy and Roman injustice *as such*, but the Lord who, by rising from the dead has proved himself to be free of the fetters of the purely local, the purely temporal, the purely human. By being born, by living a life of hard work, by loving and being loved, by suffering and dying, he associated himself with our common lot. It is for us to strive to associate ourselves with him in his more-than-human role.

This, of course, is something that cannot be achieved without that more-than-human assistance which is technically labelled by theologians the grace of God, the free gift, the assistance offered to us *gratis* by the divine benevolence. Yet, although the problem of reconciling human freedom with such grace is one that has teased the minds of theologians ever since the days of St Augustine, it is of the first importance to recognize the truth of the tag that 'grace perfects nature'. It is so often thought of as a sort of alien element injected into the human will to persuade or even compel it to do something it does not particularly want to do. 'No, grace does not force man to enter another universe; it introduces him into an extension of our own universe.'[31]

This alleged 'dualism' of the natural and supernatural orders is an idea that has been not only one of

31. Letter of 1919.

the elements of Christian teaching which has led the humanist to a rejection of religious belief; it has influenced the thought of a number of contemporary theologians. Admittedly, a writer like Dr John Robinson, author of *Honest to God*, seems to imagine that the idea of a supernatural order is tied up with what he calls the 'whole world-view' of the Bible, which is 'unashamedly supranaturalistic'. The fact that he insists on using the term *supranatural* in place of the commoner form *supernatural* may be either a cause or an effect of the confusion. But confusion there is. The term 'supernatural' has absolutely nothing to do with any spatial imagery, any more than have the terms 'upper classes' or 'higher powers' (whether in mathematics or politics). It simply refers to that order of reality—call it 'deeper', 'richer', 'fuller'—which is other than, however intimately associated with, the world of our purely human experience.

It is only too true that, as we have already seen, much of the so-called 'spiritual' writing in the Church has, to use Robinson's simile, treated those two orders as if they were like oil and water, one superimposed on the other but never interpenetrating it. The doctrine of the incarnate Word once again shows how false such a presentation is. In Christ, divine and human are two 'powers' which are yet genuinely blended in one entity, the human capacities becoming the vehicle for the action, which is therefore at once human and divine, 'theandric' to use the technical theological term. But, unless one accepts the effective presence in Christ of a power which is more than human, super-human, supernatural, one ceases to believe in the Incarnation.

Some of Teilhard's critics have indeed suggested that he did not really believe in a supernatural order at all. This is false.

> In the beginning was *Power*, intelligent, loving, ener-
> gizing. In the beginning was the *Word*, supremely
> capable of mastering and moulding whatever might
> come into being in the world of matter.[32]

Only so, as he held, could the whole cosmic process find its goal.

> . . . because the term towards which the earth is
> moving lies not merely beyond each individual thing
> but beyond the totality of things; because the world
> travails, not to bring forth from within itself some
> supreme reality, but to find its consummation through
> a union with a pre-existent being; it follows that
> man can never reach the blazing centre of the universe
> simply by living more and more for himself nor even
> by spending his life in the service of some earthly cause
> however great.[33]

'The Mass on the World' from which the foregoing passage is taken, culminates in this stupendous prayer:

> . . . dominated as I am by a vocation which springs
> from the inmost fibres of my being, I have no desire, I
> have no ability, to proclaim anything except the
> innumerable prolongations of your incarnate being in
> the world of matter; I can preach only the mystery
> of your flesh, you the soul shining forth through all
> that surrounds us.
>
> It is to your body in this its fullest extension—that
> is, to the world become through your power and my
> faith the glorious living crucible in which everything

32. *Hymn of the Universe*, p. 21; Fontana, p. 21.
33. Ibid., p. 31; Fontana, p. 29.

melts away in order to be born anew; it is to this
that I dedicate myself with all the resources which
your creative magnetism has brought forth in me: with
the all too feeble resources of my scientific knowledge, with my religious vows, with my priesthood, and
(most dear to me) with my deepest human convictions.
It is in this dedication, Lord Jesus, I desire to live,
in this I desire to die.[34]

It is easy to say that Teilhard was liable to become drunk
with words, that his language tended to outstrip his
thought and to do violence both to sanity and to orthodoxy. Yet it is impossible, if one reads him without
preconceived ideas, not to sense that he is attempting to
state a truth which is of profound significance for
any Christian believer. No one in the whole range of
Christian literature has more effectively suggested the
depths and the heights of the mystery of Christ, 'until,
knowing the love of Christ which is beyond all knowledge, you are filled with the utter fullness of God'
(Ephesians 3:19).

3

MARY

The world's energies and substances—so har-
moniously adapted and controlled that the supreme
Transcendent would seem to germinate entirely
from their immanence—concentrated and were
purified in the stock of Jesse; from their ac-

34. Ibid., pp. 36-7; Fontana, p. 35.

*cumulated and distilled treasures they produced
the glittering gem of matter, the Pearl of the
Cosmos, and the link with the incarnate personal
Absolute—the blessed Virgin Mary, Queen and
Mother of all things, the true Demeter . . .*[1]

*Nothing in the world is more intensely alive and
active than purity and prayer, which hang like
an unmoving light between the universe and God.
Through their serene transparency flow the waves
of creative power charged with natural virtue and
with grace. What else but this is the blessed
Virgin Mary?*[2]

There is a passage in *De Ecclesia*, the Second Vatican
Council's Dogmatic Constitution on the Church, which
serves as an admirable introduction to our next consideration, which is that of Teilhard's teaching on
the Mother of God and the Church of Christ:

In the mystery of the Church, herself rightly called
mother and virgin, the Blessed Virgin Mary stands out
in eminent and unique manner as exemplar of both
virginity and motherhood.

In one of his most poetic pieces, written in 1918,[3] a piece
which his great interpreter Père de Lubac has described
as a love-poem, he seeks to expound the role of woman
in his view of reality. He begins by adapting to his
purpose the passage from the book of Proverbs which
the Church has traditionally applied to Our Lady,

The Lord created me before all his works . . . I was

1. 'Cosmic Life', *Writings in Time of War*, p. 59.
2. 'The Mystical Milieu', *Writings in Time of War*, p. 144.
3. 'The Eternal Feminine', *Writings in Time of War*, pp. 192 ff.

beside him like a master workman . . . Rejoicing in
his inhabited world, and delighting in the sons of
men.

Teilhard thinks first of all of the activity of union, of the
coming together of diverse elements to produce a new
form of being. This is not yet to be seen in terms of
a personal reality; rather is it the principle that runs right
through God's creative work. For, as he repeatedly says
in his writing, *Deus creat uniendo*, it is by uniting that
God pursues his creative activity. So,

Everything in the universe is made by union and
generation—by the coming together of elements that
seek out one another, melt together two by two, and
are born again in a third.[4]

The whole passage is highly reminiscent of the opening
of Lucretius' *De Rerum Natura*, with its invocation to
Venus, 'delight of gods and men'.

In me is seen that side of beings by which they are
joined as one, in me the fragrance that makes them
hasten together and leads them, freely and passionately,
along their road to unity. . . .

I am the beauty running through the world, to make
it associate in ordered groups; the ideal held up
before the world to make it ascend.

I am the essential Feminine.

In the beginning I was no more than a mist, rising
and falling . . .

And yet I was already in existence. . . .

I was the bond that . . . held together the foun-
dations of the universe.

For every monad, be it never so humble . . . obeys
in its movement an embryo of love for me.[5]

4. Ibid., p. 192.   5. Ibid., pp. 192-3.

Soon the argument moves to the level of human love, the love of a man for a woman.

> When a man loves a woman he thinks at first that his love is given simply to an individual like himself whom he envelops in his power and freely associates with himself. . . .
>
> Soon, however, he is astonished by the violence of the forces unleashed in him at my approach . . .
>
> He thought that it was simply a partner who stood by his side: and now he sees that in me he meets the great hidden force, the mysterious latency, that has come to him in this form in order to lead him captive. . . .
>
> He who takes me, gives himself to me, and is himself taken by the universe.
>
> In the knowledge of me, alas, there is both good and evil. . . .
>
> I was at once his strength and his weakness—his hope and his trial. . . .
>
> Indeed, had Christ not come, man might well have placed me for ever in the camp of evil. . . .
>
> Christ has given me salvation and freedom. . . .
>
> The true union, however, is the union that simplifies, and to simplify is to spiritualize.
>
> The true fertility is the fertility that brings beings together in the engendering of Spirit.[6]

Much of this may seem, at a first hearing, to have little or nothing to do with what we normally understand by 'spirituality'. It is, in fact, fundamental to an understanding of Teilhard's whole ascetic, devotional and religious life. For him, unless one's higher activities, of whatever kind, were rooted and seen to be rooted in the

6. Ibid., pp. 194-7.

whole cosmic process, they were lacking that solid
ground that would enable them to grow and flourish
in any situation. As he was to say towards the end of his
life:

> Is it not becoming more obvious every day that, for
> our generation, there is something essential lacking to
> a sub-manichean Gospel, in which advances in know-
> ledge and technology are still presented, not as a
> primary co-condition of the spirituality of man, but as
> some sort of extra?[7]

It is in accordance with this basic principle of his whole
teaching that he has thus been tracing back to its
origins 'at the beginning of time' that 'feminine' strain
in the world which finds its culmination, as we shall see,
both in the Mother of God and in the Church, which
he, along with his fellow-Catholics, saw as also his
Mother.

That much being said, we can take up again the
thread of his teaching about the role of woman in the
spiritualizing of mankind. Woman remains essentially
herself, even in the light of Christian truth, but her
vocation is nobler and more sublime.

> While my deceptive image continues to lure the
> pleasure-seeker towards matter, my reality has risen
> aloft, drawing men to the heights: it floats between
> the Christian and his God.

> My charm can still draw men, but towards the
> light. I can still carry them with me, but into freedom.

> Henceforth my name is Virginity.

> The Virgin is still woman and mother ...

> Christ has left me all my jewels.

> In addition, however, he has sent down upon me

7. E. Rideau, op. cit., p. 318.

from heaven a ray that has boundlessly idealized me.[8]

The juxtaposition of the words Virgin and Mother prepares us for the final stage of his meditation. But the passage leading up to the dénouement is a remarkable statement of a profound theological truth clothed in the language of sheer poetry.

Long before I drew you, I drew God towards me.

Long before man had measured the extent of my power . . . the Lord had conceived me, whole and entire, in his wisdom, and I had won his heart.

Without the lure of my purity, think you, would God ever have come down, as flesh, to dwell in his creation?

Only love has the power to move being.

If God, then, was to be able to emerge from himself, he had first to lay a pathway of desire before his feet, he had to spread before him a sweet savour of beauty. . . .

Now do you understand the secret of the emotion that possesses you when I come near?

The tender compassion, the hallowed charm, that radiate from Woman—so naturally that it is only in her that you look for them, and yet so mysteriously that you cannot say whence they come—are the presence of God making itself felt and setting you ablaze.

Lying between God and the earth, as a zone of mutual attraction, I draw them both together in a passionate union.[9]

Bold words indeed, yet what an insight they give into the mystery of Mary and her role in the world's re-

8. 'The Eternal Feminine', op. cit., pp. 197-8. 9. Ibid., p. 200.

demption. In rather more sober language, he expresses essentially the same idea in *Le Milieu Divin*:

> When the time had come when God resolved to realize his Incarnation before our eyes, he had first of all to raise up in the world a virtue capable of drawing him as far as ourselves. He needed a mother who would engender him in the human sphere. What did he do? He created the Virgin Mary, that is to say he called forth on earth a purity so great that, within this transparency, he would concentrate himself to the point of appearing as a child.[10]

The subtle richness of this conception is so great that it needs some further investigation. Once again, it seems necessary to complain of much conventional language about the role of Mary in the economy of the Incarnation, implying as it does that she was little more than an animate tool, a passive recipient of the grace of God which drove her on to the pre-ordained acceptance of her destiny. Yet, unless the Church is wholly at fault in lauding her greatness, in emphasizing the sheerly human perfection that was hers, we are compelled to see in her a totally free, utterly responsible, active collaborator with the divine purpose. It was because she was wholly responsive to the grace that was offered to her that she was able to rise to the heights of human potentiality, to become fit for her mission, which was nothing less than the formation of the physical organism, the human body-soul that was to be, in a unique sense, the temple of God.

Even Teilhard's own language, when he talks of God's 'calling forth on earth a purity so great that, within this transparency, he would concentrate himself to

10. Op. cit., p. 125; Fontana, p. 134.

the point of appearing as a child' may still leave the
impression that the action was totally from God's side, a
kind of creation *ex nihilo*. But the truth would seem to
be that the long history of mankind prior to the
moment of the Annunciation must be thought of as a
process of education, of spiritualization of man's religious
concepts, brought about through man's chequered response to the divine guidance. In the milieu from which
Mary came, the group of men and women of whom we
have glimpses in the first two chapters of Luke's
Gospel, that process was coming to its term. In Mary it
found its apogee. Mary's *fiat* was the supreme expression of human freedom, the willingness to co-operate
with God himself. The rest of us are to a greater or
less extent opaque to the divine light. Mary was totally
translucent, so that it could, through her, shine into
a darkened world, totally undimmed. One of the titles
which the Church confers on Mary is *Porta Coeli*, gateway to heaven. It is no exaggeration to say that, from
God's side, she was the gateway to earth.

> . . . when the day of the Virgin came to pass, then
> the final purpose of the universe, deep-rooted and
> gratuitous, was suddenly made clear: since the days
> when the first breath of individualization passed over
> the expanse of the *Supreme Centre here below*, so that
> in it could be seen the ripple of the smile of the
> original monads, all things were moving towards the
> child born of woman.[11]

In a letter to his cousin, written for the feast of the
Immaculate Conception in 1916 he has this to say:

> For me the Immaculate Conception is the feast of
> 'passive action', the action that functions simply by the

11. 'Cosmic Life', op. cit., p. 59.

transmission through us of divine energy. Purity, in spite of outward appearances, is essentially an active virtue, because it concentrates God in us and on those who are subject to our influence. In Our Lady, all modes of lower, restless activity disappear within this single, luminous function of drawing God to oneself, of receiving him and letting him penetrate one's being. To be active in such a way and to such a degree, Our Lady must have been brought into existence in the very heart of grace.[12]

Mary, then, is not only the Mother of God, she is the Mother of all mankind, the Second Eve, mother of all the living that live now not merely a natural life, but that higher life of grace that comes to us through Christ.

But, within the economy of Christ's redemptive activity, that life comes to us also through his Church. So Teilhard sees the Church, too, at the culminating point of the long process of evolution from the primeval chaos. As God became Man in and through Mary, so Christ, in and through his bride, the Church, comes to individual men in all her manifold activity. Not that Teilhard was blind to the defects of the Church in her existential reality; nevertheless he remained ever conscious of the deeper reality of what she essentially is—the consciously enChristed portion of the world, the main focus-point at which the affinities that link men together meet in a more-than charity, the central axis of universal convergence, the precise meeting-point emerging between the cosmos and Omega. And again, in a time of spiritual anguish in 1925, he writes in a letter: 'I believe in and I love the Church as mediatrix between God and the

12. *The Making of a Mind*, p. 149.

world.' In an earlier letter he had already written: 'I hope with the help of God, never to do anything contrary to the Church, for outside her I can see no life-current that has any chance of success.' Nor was this conviction the outcome of any mere wishful thinking, an accommodation of his faith to his scientific views, or a kind of delusion which distorted his Christian vision, making it no more than a merely natural, humanistic response to a purely this-world phenomenon. It is true that he did, at the end of *The Phenomenon of Man*, speak of the Christian phenomenon, precisely because he was trying to show what lay behind the façade of ecclesiastical forms. He recognized that 'it is not given to everyone immediately to arrive at supernatural views of the Incarnation'. So it was desirable to be able to introduce such men to a picture of the Church which, valid in its own right as a purely historical phenomenon, might yet lead them on to a deeper understanding of what she stood for.

The Christian fact stands before us. It has its place among the other realities of the world.

I would like to show how it seems to me to bring to the perspectives of a universe dominated by energies of a personal nature the crucial confirmation we are in need of . . .

To those who know it outwardly, Christianity seems desperately intricate. In reality . . . it contains an extremely simple and yet astonishingly bold solution of the world . . . Those who fail to see in it the most cosmic of beliefs and hopes, completely fail to understand its 'mysteries'. Is the kingdom of God a big family? Yes, in a sense it is. But in another sense it is a prodigious biological operation—that of the redeeming Incarnation.[13]

Lest the term 'biological operation' be interpreted as laying Teilhard open to a charge of ignoring or denying the reality of the action of grace in this task, let us remind ourselves, first of all, that he is using the sort of language that might be meaningful to the unbeliever, whilst it provides a sort of metaphor which even the believer could find helpful. That he was fully aware of man's need of grace and of its vitalizing presence in the world, many a passage can testify. He never tired of insisting on man's responsibility to act, to make his contribution to the perfecting of the creative process, yet he was equally clear that:

> Every human enrichment, no matter what it be, is but dust unless, by uniting itself to a centre of immortal love, it becomes the most precious and incorruptible of all things. So again: I attribute no final and absolute value to the various constructions man has built up . . . What I love in them is not their function; and that is, in some mysterious way, to construct first what can be divinized and then through the grace of Christ that adds itself to our effort, to construct the divine.[14]

Returning, then, to Teilhard's view of the Church, we see him insisting that, in his view, what Christ is doing in and through the Church is to unite the personal and the universal. Himself a person, Christ gives to the world of personal beings their infinite value, since it is,

13. *The Phenomenon of Man* (Collins, London, and Harper & Row, New York, 1959), pp. 292-3; Fontana, pp. 320-1.
14. E. Rideau, op. cit., p. 198.

in the end, from our knowledge of him that we come to appreciate what personality is. In all other human beings it is defective, limited, dependent. The divine personality that functions in the human nature of Christ and, through him, in his Church, is the manifestation of perfection at a level beyond all that we could imagine personality to involve.

> . . . if evolution were to reach its highest point, in our small, separate lives, then indeed the enormous travail of terrestrial organization into which we are born would be no more than a tragic irrelevance. We should all be dupes. We should do better in that case to stop, to call a halt, destroy the machines, close the laboratories, and seek whatever way of escape we can find in pure pleasure or pure nirvana.[15]

Fortunately we have the teaching of the Church, the faith which, far from being a way of escaping from the world, is the leavening principle of the world's very fulfilment. 'As an instrument of evolutionary activation, the Church is unquestionably irreplaceable—and invincible.' 'Irreplaceable' because:

> *Alone*, unconditionally alone, in the world today, Christianity shows itself able to reconcile in a single living act the all and the person. Alone, it can bend our hearts not only to the service of that tremendous movement of the world which bears us along, but beyond, to embrace that movement in love.[16]

For, using the biological term *phylum*, which strictly speaking applies to one of the major subdivisions of the animal kingdom, Teilhard speaks at times of the Church as the *phylum* of love—that human group which is

15. *The Future of Man*, p. 117-18; Fontana, p. 122.
16. *The Phenomenon of Man*, p. 298; Fontana, p. 326.

distinguished from all other groups by its profession and practice of charity. Irresistibly, we are reminded of the words of the Church's own Founder: 'By this will all men know that you are my disciples, if you have love for one another.'

If this is too idealistic a picture of the Church as she is encountered in her day-to-day activities, it is at least clear what a lofty concept of the Church's authentic nature Teilhard both formed and taught.

How the Church's effective action is realized in the concrete is, of course, primarily through her sacramental dispensation, centred in the Eucharist. He sees this as both parallel to and an extension of the event of the Incarnation. Just as, at a certain moment in time and at a particular place on the world's surface, God entered into his own universe, so, when the priest takes the host into his hands and pronounces the words 'This is my body', the God-Man enters that particular speck of reality to dwell there. But, whilst this is true, it is also true that his action is not confined to that small circle. He has chosen through the vehicle of the consecrated elements to enter into, to vitalize the members of his body who are thus more closely associated with him and with one another. They all converge upon Christ, yet each remains a centre of supernatural energy. The responsibility for action remains. Speaking in the person of a priest, Teilhard says:

I know how the life-giving power of the host can be blocked by our freedom of will. If I seal up the entry into my heart I must dwell in darkness—and not only I— my individual soul—but the whole universe in so far as its activity sustains my organism and awakens my consciousness, and in so far also as I act upon it in my turn . . . But if, on the other hand, *my heart is open to you*, then at once through the pure intent of my will the divine must flood into the universe, in so far as the universe is centred on men. Since . . . I shall have become a living particle of the body of Christ, all that affects me must in the end help on the growth of the total Christ. . . .

I pray that this brief and limited contact with the sacramental species may introduce me to a universal and eternal communion with Christ, with his omni-operant will and his boundless mystical body.[17]

As a sort of footnote to what we have said about Teilhard's devotion to the Church, we may quote the passage in which he says that:

If Christianity . . . is indeed destined to be the religion of tomorrow, there is only one way in which it can hope to come up to the measure of today's great humanitarian trends and assimilate them; and that is through the axis, living and organic, of its Catholicism centred on Rome.[18]

This is far from being the bigoted and unecumenical remark it might seem to be. No one was less bigoted or more open to the appeal of sheer human goodness, whenever it might be found. 'Time and again', he says, 'life has brought me in contact with men whose activities and convictions placed them in a camp generally considered to be the opposite of my own. Between them and me, according to the recognized conventions, there should have been defiance or hostility. But instead of this coldness, a deep sympathy sprang up from the first moment of our meeting . . . Labelled as enemies, we

17. 'The Priest', *Writings in Time of War*, pp. 215-18.
18. E. Rideau, op. cit., p. 597.

at once recognized that we were brothers. And why? Simply because all we were trying to do, on either side, was to magnify and unify the earth.'[19] For he knew that anyone who, from whatever motive, was striving to magnify the earth was, however unconsciously, magnifying the Lord of the earth.

To conclude this brief study of Teilhard's thinking about Mary and about the Church, it seems desirable once again to draw attention to the fact that, for all the sublimity of his language and the wide-ranging speculation of his thought, the down-to-earth quality of his actual practice was fundamental. Not only do we have the evidence of his annual retreat notes, in which he is as careful and precise as the most unsophisticated novice might be about his daily practices—'Our Lady: angelus, rosary', 'better prepared meditation'—but we have the assurance of his colleagues about the 'extreme punctiliousness' of his religious observance.[20] Despite the difficulties which his life, whether as a chaplain during the war or as a travelling scientist, presented, difficulties which led him to develop the profound and moving meditation on the Mass on the World's Altar, he obviously preferred to be able to say mass regularly. Thus, in one letter,

> There's a fine church here, and no priest. I have no difficulty in saying mass.[21]

Equally, if it was necessary to hold public services, he liked them to be 'carried out with supreme dignity, a condition very difficult to fulfil in a country hole.'[22]

Another letter from the Front refers to 'Rosary in the

19. R. Speaight, op. cit., p. 265.
20. H. de Lubac, *The Faith of Teilhard de Chardin*, pp. 70, 79.
21. *The Making of a Mind*, p. 175.   22. Ibid., pp. 175-6.

fog' and to the 'oblation of your whole self which I was privileged to make of the one victim of the world in the little cellar-chapel at Nieuport.'[23]

On one occasion he speaks of

being deprived of the sacraments—though I have some compensation for this since I've been carrying the Blessed Sacrament on me.

Thus he can end the letter by saying

May Our Lord, who rests on my heart, bless you and grant you his joy and peace.[24]

In a letter to the Abbé Breuil, from Tientsin, in 1923:

I received the announcement of your mother's death yesterday, and I have just said mass for her and for those she has left behind . . . I pray for you daily when I ask God's protection for those who are nearest to me 'in heart, in thought, and in science'—and you are included in all three categories.[25]

Indeed, such fidelity to the minutiae of religious practice would be entirely in accord with his general principles of careful attention to detail in every aspect of life, scientific as well as personal. In an earlier quotation we have seen him appreciating the value of the most apparently trivial experiences—a sound, a sight, a look—and we can hardly doubt that he would see more rather than less meaning in the consecrated activities and gestures of traditional piety. If he sought for a 'new formulation of holiness' this would no more mean abolishing old forms than his search for a super-humanity meant an end to the traditional courtesies of civilized exchange. That would be as sensible as to wish to blot out the sun because we now have electric light.

23. Ibid., pp. 92-3.   24. Ibid., pp. 100-1.
25. *Letters from a Traveller*, pp. 103-4.

4

FULLNESS OF LIFE

In virtue of the fundamental unity of our being and the world, we may already say of every upright man that everything he does on earth is ordered more or less directly to the spiritualization of the universe.[1]

To sum up . . . neither of the two components of the interior life (growth, and then diminishment, both natural, in Christo) can or should destroy the other. There are not two opposed forms of ascesis, one of development and the other of mortification. There are two phases with a capacity to combine in a flexible and dynamic equilibrium.[2]

The saint is the man who Christianizes in himself all the human of his own time.[3]

The most explicit formulation of Teilhard's spiritual teaching is to be found in what is his most characteristic work—*Le Milieu Divin*. The title itself, which has given so much difficulty to his English translators that they have finally decided that it was untranslatable, refers to the whole cosmic picture. This is the world of God, the world that belongs to God but also the world that has to be won back for God, since it too, like mankind itself,

1. *'Forma Christi', Writings in Time of War*, p. 258.
2. Ibid., p. 263.   3. C. Cuénot, op. cit., p. 403.

is, to use Newman's phrase, involved in that 'aboriginal
calamity' which we call the fall.

'The created universe waits with eager expectation
for the revelation that God's sons are to enjoy. It became the victim of frustration . . . yet always there was
hope, because the universe itself is to be freed from the
shackles of mortality and enter into that liberty which
is to come with the glorification of God's sons. We know
that the whole created universe is still groaning through
and through as though in the pangs of childbirth. Even
we, who have received the Spirit, like the first-fruits of
a future harvest, also groan inwardly as we wait for
God to ransom our bodies by making us his sons'
(Romans 8: 19-23).

The word translated 'frustration' in the above passage
is often rendered 'vanity', as in the well-known passage:
' "Vanity of vanities," said the Preacher: "everything is
vanity" '—an idea which has influenced far too much of
our traditional spirituality. It was an idea which Teilhard
fought against all his life. In his early days as a
Jesuit, as he tells us himself, he felt that his attraction
towards nature was incompatible with his pursuit of
the 'higher life', as expounded for example in the
Imitation of Christ—a document inspired almost as
much by the ideal of Stoic *apatheia* and the pessimism of
the Preacher as by genuine Christian theology. We recall
how another Jesuit, Gerard Manley Hopkins, went even
further and not only destroyed such poetry as he had
already written but resolved to write no more, as not
belonging to his profession. It was some years before
Hopkins overcame this scruple. The young Teilhard was
more fortunate. 'At that moment', he says, 'I would
have gone off the rails if it had not been for the solid

common sense of Père Troussard. What he did, in fact, was simply to assure me that my crucified God looked for a "natural" development of my being, as well as for its sanctification.'[4]

The great lesson he was to learn—and to teach—was that such sanctification normally comes through such natural development.

For Teilhard saw clearly that the logical effect of the Incarnation, the central truth of the Christian faith, should be to make us realize that, since God has thus inserted himself into the cosmos, this has become the field of his divine supernaturalizing activity, as it is already the field of his creative energizing. Hence it follows that we human beings can become godlike only in so far as we too associate ourselves with God in his twofold action. Any suggestion that the world is, in itself, anything but essentially good is to imply that God has both created and made use of an unworthy and squalid entity. Yet, within the complex and diverse body of teaching and practice which goes by the name of Christian asceticism, there are strands which cannot be incorporated into an overall authentic Christianity. Whilst accepting, as we must, the reality of sin and evil, and the doctrine of the fall, these must never be allowed to engender in our minds an attitude that is, in effect, Manichaean in origin. Christianity has always insisted, in theory, on seeing creation with God's eyes —as something wholly good in itself. Evil, the outcome of sin, is to be attributed to the spirit of disobedience, manifesting itself at every level of created existence, from the angelic spirits who rebelled to the recalcitrant material entities which, as St Paul taught,

4. C. Cuénot, op. cit., p. 7.

are themselves somehow at odds with God's spirit.

Yet, in practice, all too often Christians have spoken and acted as though the service of God, the pursuit of sanctity could be achieved only through a denial, a refusal, a turning one's back on creation, the better to contemplate and love the Creator. The result of such an attitude of mind has been psychologically bad for many who have attempted to practise what is basically an inhumane system; it has been disastrous for the Church's apostolic mission. Reasonably enough, men have rejected a creed which seemed to teach that the ordinary interests and concerns of men were somehow at variance with, if not in opposition to, the divine purpose. For the sake of the faithful themselves as well as of those men of good will whom he encountered in many of his scientific journeys and conferences, Teilhard set out in close and detailed argument his view of what sanctification means.

He begins by analysing the dilemma in which many good souls find themselves:

> On the one hand a very sure instinct, mingled with their love for that which is . . . draws them to the joy of creating and of knowing. On the other hand a higher will to love God above all else makes them afraid of the least division or deflection in their allegiances. In the most spiritual layers of their being they experience a tension between the opposing ebb and flow caused by the drawing power of the two rival stars . . . God and the world. Which of the two is to make itself more nobly adored?[5]

5. *Le Milieu Divin*, p. 22; Fontana, p. 52; U.S. ed., p. 20.

Three alternative solutions propose themselves. The Christian will either

(a) 'force himself to confine his concern to purely religious objects' or

(b) 'he will dismiss the evangelical counsels and decide to lead what seems to him a complete and human life', or

(c) 'and this is the most usual case, he will give up any attempt to make sense of his situation; he will never belong wholly to God nor ever wholly to things; incomplete in his own eyes, and insincere in the eyes of his fellows, he will gradually acquiesce in a double life.'[5]

None of these solutions is acceptable to Teilhard.

For him the authentic Christian way is the fourth way, which consists in seeing how, without making the smallest concession to weakness or inferiority, but with a thirst for greater perfection, we can reconcile and indeed provide mutual nourishment for the love of God and a healthy love of the world, a striving towards detachment and, at the same time, a striving towards the enrichment of our human lives. But even for those who recognize that natural activity is an important aspect of our service to God, there is a danger that they may think of the value of this activity simply in terms of the intention with which it is done. This is how Teilhard pictures a certain type of director addressing his spiritual children.

> . . . you must let the clear spring-water of purity of intention flow into your work . . . Cleanse your intention, and the least of your actions will be filled with God. Certainly the material side of your actions

6. Ibid.

has no definitive value. . . . But what *will* count [in the New Jerusalem], what will always endure, is this: that you have acted in all things *conformably* to the will of God. . . . If worldly aims have no value in themselves, you can love them for the opportunity they give you of proving your faithfulness to God.[7]

Teilhard recognizes that there is much truth in this sort of language: a good intention is of paramount importance. The will of God is a fundamental factor in the whole of life. But, whilst the divinization (Teilhard's term for what is more commonly called the sanctification or consecration) of our efforts by the value of the intention put into it 'pours a priceless *soul* into all our actions . . . *it does not confer the hope of resurrection upon their bodies.*'[8] Yet that is the hope we need if our joy is to be complete. He then proceeds to state, in syllogistic form, the argument in favour of a thoroughgoing acceptance of our day-to-day activities as the very stuff of our fulfilment at the supernatural no less than at the natural level.

At the heart of our universe, each soul exists for God, in our Lord.

But all reality, even material reality, around each one of us, exists for our souls.[9]

Hence, all sensible reality, around each one of us, exists, through our souls, for God in our Lord.

No Christian can question the truth of the statement that souls exist for God, in Christ. This is a logical conclusion from the very fact of Christ's redemptive

7. Ibid., p. 24; Fontana, pp. 53-4; U.S. ed., p. 22.
8. Ibid., pp. 25-6; Fontana, p. 55; U.S. ed., p. 23.
9. Ibid., p. 27; Fontana, p. 56; U.S. ed., p. 25.

Incarnation, the fact that, in St Paul's words, God has reconciled us to himself in and through Christ. But this must not be thought of in terms of some purely extrinsic, formal, legal relationship. The whole idea of Christ's mystical body is that we become linked with him in an intimate, personal, organic unity: we are fulfilled, as ourselves, sheerly in virtue of this incorporation into the very being of the God-Man. Nor is it necessary to prove the next step in the argument, though it is important to appreciate its full meaning. We live at the centre of a complex network of natural forces, which are not merely active at the present moment to sustain our physical nature. The very food we eat comes, perhaps, from afar; the forces that have gone to produce it have been at work for indefinite ages, preparing the world for this present harvest. But what of the spiritual influences that come to me from the remote past—the ancient teachers, themselves in turn dependent on still earlier ages, and so on? It is true that the soul, the spiritual quality in man, is of transcendent importance. But modern medicine, physiology, psychology are showing how much our spiritual selves are influenced, controlled, developed by so many factors that seem, at first sight, to be no more than sheerly material. In virtue of the close kinship existing between the material and the spiritual, we have to learn to appreciate the spiritual significance of even our corporeal activities. However literally we take the idea of a special creation of each soul, it nevertheless remains patently true that, at birth and throughout life, it is inseparable from the physical world into which it is born. So that Teilhard can say:

In each soul, God loves and partly saves the whole

world which that soul sums up in an incommunicable and particular way.[10]

Yet this does not mean that man is passive under the power of God.

> [Each man] *makes his own soul* throughout all his earthly days; and at the same time he collaborates in another work . . . the completing of the world.[11]

We can now begin to appreciate not merely the conclusion of the particular argument which Teilhard is elaborating but the whole trend of his thought. Through our human activities whereby we seek to transform our allotted sphere, our particular area of the cosmic whole, Christ is at work in us 'divinizing' our activities and so divinizing the world.

> With each of our *works*, we labour to . . . bring to Christ a little fulfilment.[12]

Pausing for a moment to point out how mistaken are those good souls who think of man's work as a sort of spiritual obstacle, feeling that the time spent in the office or the factory or the studio is time taken away from the important duties of prayer and adoration, he repeats that, by virtue of the creation and still more of the Incarnation, '*nothing* here below is *profane* for those who know how to see'.[13] For God

> is not far away from us, altogether apart from the world we see, touch, hear, smell and taste about us. . . . There is a sense in which he is at the tip of my pen, my spade, my brush, my needle—of my heart and of my thought. By pressing the stroke, the line, or the

10. Ibid., p. 32; Fontana, p. 60; U.S. ed., p. 29.
11. Ibid.; Fontana, p. 61.
12. Ibid., p. 34; Fontana, p. 62; U.S. ed., p. 31.
13. Ibid., p. 38; Fontana, p. 66; U.S. ed., p. 35.

stitch . . . to its ultimate natural finish, I shall lay hold of that last end towards which my innermost will tends.[14]

What Teilhard, then, is preaching is nothing less than an authentic Christian humanism, the answer to those who reject Christianity because it does not lead its followers to levels of achievement beyond our ordinary human powers but rather withdraws them from the common task of humanity. No, says Teilhard, the true Christian can recognize and accept every sort of human and humane value and must do all he can to preserve and develop it by incorporating it into its source and final end, Christ, supreme man, incarnate deity.

At the same time, Teilhard would take issue with the agnostic humanist, who has no explanation in his philosophy for the ever-present fact of suffering and evil of different kinds. In the second section of *Le Milieu Divin* he addresses himself to this problem, discussing the sanctification of our sufferings, and of those other experiences in which we play a passive rather than active role. It is sometimes said that Teilhard's optimism was such that he seemed blind to the realities of sin and suffering in the world. The truth is that he was intensely alive to suffering and to evil of every kind, even if his vision of the great plan of God's redeeming love enabled him to look beyond the present to a glorious future. Indeed, it seems not unreasonable to urge that it was precisely because he was so well aware of the dark side of life that he was driven to find an answer, an explanation, a reconciliation of what he saw with what he believed. He might well have quoted Milton's appeal:

14. Ibid., p. 37; Fontana, p. 64; U.S. ed., pp. 33-4.

> *What in me is dark*
> *Illumine, what is low raise and support;*
> *That to the height of this great argument*
> *I may assert eternal providence*
> *And justify God's ways to man.*[15]

The moment has come, he says, to plumb the decidedly negative side of our lives—the side on which, however far we search, we cannot discern any happy result, or any solid conclusion to what happens to us. 'It is easy enough to understand that God can be grasped in and through every life. But can God also be found in and through every death?'[16] Let us ask ourselves how our apparent deaths, that is to say the waste-matter of our existences, can find their place in the establishment of God's kingdom and God's *milieu*. Part of the answer lies in the fact that the very evils in the world are a summons and a challenge to us to co-operate with God in their elimination. At the very first approach of anything that may diminish, in myself or in others, that fullness of life and being which is God's purpose for me, I can find God only by loathing what is coming and doing my best to avoid it. The more we repel suffering the more closely we cleave to God. And here, perhaps, it is relevant to recall that Christ himself, faced with his Passion, prayed that he might be spared the drinking of the bitter cup. Nevertheless, as we know, he accepted it as his Father's will. What does this mean?

The world being what it is, a world in process of becoming, a world that has not yet been perfected, there

15. *Paradise Lost*, Book I, p. 22.
16. *Le Milieu Divin*, p. 59; Fontana, p. 80; U.S. ed., p. 52.

must inevitably be found in it failures, threats, disappointments, suffering—all those features of life which we would gladly escape but which are, as we say, the common lot of men. It is not that God wills them directly. He permits them it is true, in virtue of the need to respect man's choices and not to *impose* on a recalcitrant world the healing which it constantly rejects. Yet he is ever at hand to convert evil into good, with our co-operation. There are many cases in which we can actually see how this happens—the missed opportunity which turns out to have been, as we say, 'providential', the occasions for courage, self-sacrifice, patience, charity, and other virtues which might remain 'unexercised and unbreathed' in a less challenging world. But for all that, there remain all too many cases where the human mind is baffled and human hearts are broken —it would seem pointlessly. Here it is only the message of the Cross that has any value.

Yet we must not think of the Cross negatively and destructively. 'Far too often', says Teilhard, 'the Cross is presented for our adoration, not so much as a sublime end to be attained by our transcending ourselves, but as a symbol of sadness, of limitation and repression.'[17] He would agree wholeheartedly with those recent developments in the Church's theological, liturgical and spiritual teaching which insist that the Cross should not be seen in isolation, separated from the triumph of the Resurrection. Since Christ, God incarnate, has taken upon himself a human destiny, has suffered and died and *risen again*, Christianity means that the term of creation is not to be found in the purely temporal and visible, but

17. Ibid., p. 85; Fontana, p. 102; U.S. ed., p. 76.

that the effort required of us in our fidelity to Christ is to be consummated in a way and in a world beyond any this-world transformation of ourselves and of everything about us. This is where a purely this-world humanism fails us. In terms of a purely empirical philosophy, a philosophy that refuses to admit the possibility, still less the reality, of a world of being beyond this present tangible order of things, suffering and, above all, death present the final scandal, the ultimate stumbling-block to hope.

But the Cross, with its obverse and fulfilment, the Resurrection, means that, to find the complete truth and the total explanation, we must pass beyond the frontiers of the world of sense and of all the limitation that that world implies. It is here that the 'folly' of the Cross presents itself to those 'wise men' who are not prepared to stake the good they hold in their hands at the moment on what lies 'beyond'. 'The royal road of the Cross' is neither more nor less than the road of human endeavour supernaturally righted and prolonged. So we see that Teilhard's 'optimism' is no facile and superficial anodyne. Nor would he seek to water down the stern teaching of so many masters of the spiritual life, as they summon their disciples to self-discipline and renunciation. But what he would plead is that we should see these necessary 'passivities' in the context of that total fulfilment of the Christian ascetic whereby he makes his contribution to the fulfilment of the total Christ.

That Christ may enter deeply into us we need alternately the work that widens our being and the sorrow that brings death to it, the life that makes a man greater in order that he may be sanctifiable and the death that makes him less in order that he may be sanctified.[18]

Perhaps the most precise and explicit treatment of the problem raised by suffering is to be found in an article he wrote in 1933, addressed directly to a group of suffering men and women.[19] He begins by explaining how we should understand the process by which the world is being built. It is wrong to think of it as a sort of vast flower-bed, planted arbitrarily according to the casual whim of some celestial gardener. In that case, our place and our role in it would depend simply on his incomprehensible decision. Rather must we think of ourselves, not as flowers picked, cut and arranged in a bouquet, but as the leaves or blossoms of a growing tree, appearing in accordance with the plan, the purpose and the needs of the whole. In this total plan, each constituent element has its unique role to play. The role of the healthy individual is easy to accept. But what contribution can the sufferer make?

Reverting to his simile, he points out that, in a bunch of flowers, you would not expect to find imperfect specimens. But in a growing tree, owing to the accidents of weather or other adverse conditions, there are liable to be bruised or broken twigs, branches, blossoms. So it is in a universe in travail. Varying his comparison, he likens human beings to soldiers thrown into a battle. The achievement of victory is the aim of the commander; but that achievement is invariably bought at the price of human suffering.

Sufferers of whatever species are the expression of this

18. 'The Priest', *Writings in Time of War*, p. 209.
19. 'The Significance of the Positive Value of Suffering', *Human Energy*, pp. 48 ff.

stern but noble condition. They are not useless and dwarfed. They are simply paying for the forward march and triumph of all. They are casualties, fallen on the field of honour.[20]

It must be confessed that there is something a little facile and almost heartless about this line of thought; but when he turns to the more specifically religious argument, his message becomes more encouraging. Making use of the Christian doctrine of the mystical body, he recalls St Paul's words about the functions of the different members and parts of the total organism. In the total striving towards a fuller life, a more complete fulfilment of the whole community of men in Christ, there will be a place for every type of human energizing, every kind of human experience. Precisely because healthy humanity is in real danger of resting in the enjoyment of the good things of life, without rising above them to the thought of what lies beyond the immediate present, the contribution of the sick and maimed is of paramount importance. Without simply acquiescing in his condition, taking every opportunity that presents itself of alleviating his suffering, using such strength as still remains to him in such tasks as he can perform, the patient can yet continue to recognize that his very frustration can be fruitful and genuinely constructive. For even suffering represents potential energy.

> In suffering the ascending force of the world is concealed in a very intense form. The whole question is how to liberate and give it a consciousness of its significance and potentialities.[21]

The answer is to be found in the spiritual energy which

20. Ibid., p. 50.   21. Ibid., p. 51.

the sufferer can still deploy. The joint desire of all the sufferers in the whole world, the sheer union of mutual sympathy and conscious striving towards the purification and strengthening of man's corporate effort could be genuine and positive achievement.

Would not this be one of the highest forms that the mysterious work of creation could take in our sight?

Could it not be precisely for this that the creation was completed in Christian eyes by the Passion of Jesus? On the cross, we are perhaps in danger of seeing only an individual suffering, a single act of expiation. The creative power of that death escapes us.[22]

Yet our Christian faith tells us that through this suffering, this death, the final joy, the fullness of life, was brought to mankind. This, it is true, is an argument that can appeal only to the believer. Yet might not that believer's faith be, in itself, a kind of symbol of mankind's aspirations?

Even from the earthly point of view, the crucified Jesus, fully understood, is not rejected or conquered. It is on the contrary he who bears the weight and draws ever higher towards God the universal march of progress.[23]

Whether or not we accept the line of argumentation, at least we must admit that Teilhard was well aware of the problem and brought to an attempted solution all the resources of his compassionate heart and his religious faith.

A more important problem—more important, that is, from a purely speculative point of view, if felt as less agonizing—is that concerning the presence of moral evil in the world. It is not too difficult to see that, granted

22. Ibid., pp. 51-2.   23. Ibid., p. 52.

the idea that evolutionary progress is achieved through some sort of struggle, then there will be loss, destruction, physical dislocation. It might, it is true, be suggested that, since evolution is a natural process, it should come about as effortlessly and painlessly as a flower unfolds. In his discussion of suffering, Teilhard used the simile of a tree that is damaged through adverse weather conditions. The question may still be asked, why should the conditions within which the whole evolutionary process occurs be in any way adverse? If 'spirit' is a kind of efflorescence of matter, why should its origins be accompanied by such violent birth-pangs?

Perhaps, then, the problem of suffering is simply one aspect, in a sense a more superficial aspect, of a deeper mystery—the mystery of any sort of evil in a world in process of self-development. Certainly, St Paul would see the whole of the cosmos as affected by some universal defect, involving not just mankind but, it would seem, all that exists. 'Creation still retains the hope of being freed, like us, from its slavery to decadence, to enjoy the same freedom and glory as the children of God. From the beginning until now the entire creation, as we know, has been groaning in one great act of giving birth . . .' (Romans 8 : 21-2).

In various essays, some of them unpublished, Teilhard has wrestled with this problem. Reduced to its simplest elements, his answer would seem to be somewhat as follows. The ideal state of affairs is one of complete and harmonious unity, not a static and undifferentiated unity, but a unity of balanced forces, working together in a dynamism that is at once fruitful and fulfilled. The ideal is, of course, realized in the triune God, perfect in unity, yet enjoying the richness of interpersonal communion. In choosing to create, God creates out of love, out of a desire to call into existence an order of reality which might share, in its own measure, in the perfection of the Godhead. Since this order of reality is, of its very nature and by definition, created, it cannot share in the perfection of God fully and completely. Indeed it would seem that God's creative design is to implant within the universe a power of self-realization which is a kind of reflection of the eternal self-fulfilment of his own being.

But, at the level of created being, such a power is necessarily limited, inadequate, feeble, by comparison with the omnipotence, the wisdom, the sheer goodness of the Creator. Whilst, then, on the positive side it contains within itself the potentiality of final achievement and success, it contains also the possibility of failure. Perhaps not even omnipotence can create a world which is bound to succeed. Certainly, in so far as God has endowed man with freedom similar to though immeasurably less complete than his own, he risks the possibility of disaster. Perfect freedom, as it exists in the Godhead, is incapable of anything but good, as Augustine insists. Human freedom is far short of perfect; it is capable of wrong choices, and this capability has, in fact, resulted in disastrously wrong choices. The involvement of man in the onward movement of the development of the universe, an involvement the extent of which we are just beginning to recognize, presumably reached far beyond the phenomenal level. Man's mastery over nature, symbolized in the Bible story by the action of God in bringing 'all the wild beasts and all the birds of heaven' to see what man would call them, may well imply a far deeper and more significant relationship than we realize. Even at the sheerly empirical level we are learning how man's selfishness and greed can lead to pollution and waste of the earth's resources. May it not be that the affinity between matter and spirit is so close that the latter's failure reacts on the former, to produce the natural cataclysms and ravaging diseases,

> . . . the thousand natural shocks
> that flesh is heir to.

Thus moral evil and physical suffering would turn out to be two sides of the same medal, two aspects of one dis-ordered reality, a state of disunion and disintegra-tion. For, as Teilhard constantly insists *Deus creat uniendo*, creative achievement comes through unity. Evil then is disunity, incoherence, some degree of chaos. Certainly at the moral level it is manifestly true that much sin springs from a refusal to collaborate, to unite with others, from a determination to go one's own way, to turn inwards rather than outwards towards others; in the end from a refusal to love. Physical evil of any kind, but especially suffering, arises in a situation where the elements involved are not co-ordinated and controlled by some overriding impulse which directs them to a constructive, health-giving, *total* good.

> Initially, we must see the formative energy of the world as grappling with an infinite tendency to crumble into dust, with a thing that is by its nature (and hence by its general trend) infinitely dissociated, a sort of pure multiple. The problem and the secret of creation consisted in reducing this power of dissocia-tion and reversing its direction, in such a way as to produce progressively more synthesized monads.[24]

The problem remains, now at the deepest level. Why

24. 'Creative Union', *Writings in Time of War*, p. 155.

should there be present at the origin of things this 'thing' which is 'infinitely dissociated'? The Gnostics and Manichees, as we have seen, solved the problem by postulating a sort of Counter-God; what, in Teilhardian terms, we might describe as a principle of dissociation, sheer inert matter, overcome by the power of spirit, the creative, unifying force of God. This solution is not open to the Christian who believes in the God without whom there is nothing at all. Why, then, in creating, does God cause to exist a state of affairs, the 'formless void' of the Genesis account, which needs to be reduced to order?

Here, of course, we are face to face with one of the ultimate metaphysical puzzles, the mystery of what we mean by creation 'out of nothing'. In a statement of his basic creed, written in 1948, he has this to say:

> The self-subsistent unity lies at the pole of being, and as a necessary consequence the multiple occupies the whole circumference around it—I mean that *pure* multiple: 'Creatable nothingness', which is nothing, and yet, in virtue of a passive potentiality for arrangement (that is to say, union), is at the same time a possibility of, or a yearning for, being . . .[25]

It has to be admitted that this is much more poetical than strictly metaphysical. Perhaps it only serves to bring out the darkness of the mystery. But at least it makes two things clear. First of all, to suggest, as some have done, that Teilhard was somewhat light-hearted in his treatment of evil, whether physical or moral, is quite unjust. It may be said that, on the contrary, it was one of his major preoccupations. In the second place, it serves to underline the doctrine of 'creative union' as

25. E. Rideau, op. cit., p. 507.

a major theme in all his work. This, again, is no mere metaphysical speculation. It is true that Teilhard applies it first of all to the process of evolution itself, which he sees as the ever-growing unification of separate monads or lesser groupings into larger and more harmonious entities. But it applies also in the human and moral sphere, with his insistence on the all-importance of genuine, creative love, both as between individuals and as between groups. The curious term 'amorization' of which he is almost too fond is the stage beyond 'hominization', the development of human beings simply as human beings. To fulfil themselves as persons, to complete the destiny of mankind as a whole, human beings need that outward-looking, outward-going, generous response to the needs of others which will unite them in a common effort for the total well-being of the family and of the world.

It will be clear from this analysis that, whatever the theoretical value of his speculation may be, the practical implications of his teaching are incontestable. The traditional insistence on the virtue we call charity or love as the greatest of the three qualities through which man orders aright his attitude to God, receives a powerful impulse from the vision which relates it not simply to the immediate situation but to the larger context of man's universal mission. The texts which have become almost clichés—'overcome evil by good' (Romans 12:21), 'hatred provokes disputes, love covers over all offences' (Proverbs 10:12)—take on a fresh meaning in the light of the Teilhardian doctrines of genuinely creative union.

III

A Faith for
the Twentieth Century

*I mean by 'faith' any adherence of our intelligence
to a general view of the universe . . . To believe
is to effect an intellectual synthesis.*[1]

*The World (its value, its infallibility and its good-
ness)—that, when all is said and done, is the
first, the last, and the only thing in which I
believe.*[2]

*A general convergence of religions upon a univer-
sal Christ who fundamentally satisfies them all:
that seems to me the only possible conversion of
the world, and the only form in which a religion
of the future can be conceived.*[3]

As we come to the end of this study of the spirituality of
Teilhard de Chardin, a study which has ranged widely
over his voluminous writings, it will be helpful to draw
together and summarize the essentials of his teaching. As
we have seen, however vast the scope of his vision, it
derived ultimately from the traditional teaching and
practice of the faith in which he had been nurtured. Faith
in God, devotion to Christ in the Holy Eucharist
and in his Sacred Heart, love of the Mother of God, the
practice of the Christian virtues—charity, purity, self-
sacrifice—these are the familiar elements of Catholic piety

1. *How I Believe*, p. 9.   2. Ibid., p. 11.   3. Ibid., p. 41.

at any level. Yet he saw that the very familiarity of these notions was in danger of impoverishing their value and weakening their inspiration. Moreover, he was only too conscious of the fact that the traditional presentation of many Christian truths was no longer meaningful, let alone attractive, to men whose world-picture was so different from that of the ages during which such a presentation had been developed and for which, possibly, it was satisfactory. What he sought to produce was a statement of Christian belief and ascetic practice which would do justice at once to the Church's authentic traditions and to the convictions of twentieth-century man. When Pope John XXIII opened the Second Vatican Council more than seven years after Teilhard's death, he used words which are redolent of Teilhard's spirit:

> The spirit of the whole world is looking for a step forward towards a deeper penetration of doctrine and a development of human consciousness in complete and faithful conformity with orthodox teaching; but this teaching must be studied and presented through the methods of research and in the linguistic forms of modern thought. The substance of the old teaching of the deposit of faith is one thing; the way in which it is presented is another.

It was precisely in this spirit that Teilhard worked. 'There are many reasonable men', he said, 'who honestly consider and denounce Christian resignation as being one of the most dangerous and soporific elements in the "opium of the people". . . . this accusation, or even suspicion, is infinitely more effective, at this moment, in preventing the conversion of the world than all the objections drawn from science or philosophy. A religion that is judged to be inferior to our human idea . . . is already *condemned*.'[4]

Hence it was necessary to reformulate the traditional ascetic teaching of the Church in a way which takes account of all men's present achievements and present concerns. Scientific discoveries, technological developments, the haunting picture of an ever-expanding universe, the widespread sensitivity to the violence of a world in upheaval—these facts had presented the Christian with a problem which, if not new in kind, called for an answer formulated in new terms. ' "Christian" and "Human" ', he declared, 'are tending to drift apart. This is the great schism that now threatens the Church.'[5]

> On one side we have . . . an innate, tumultuous, surge of cosmic and humanitarian aspirations, whose rise cannot be checked, but which are dangerously imprecise and still more dangerously 'impersonal' in their expression: the new faith in the world. And, on the other side, we have . . . the vision and expectation of a universal pole, transcendent and loving: the ancient faith in God. On one side, in the form of modern humanism, we have a sort of neo-paganism, bursting with life but still lacking a head; on the other side, in the form of Christianity, a head in which the circulation of the blood has slowed down . . . Can we possibly fail to see that these two halves are designed to be combined into one whole?[6]

And again:

> We are not offering a Christianity of the requisite quality for the world to be enriched by it . . . What

4. *Le Milieu Divin*, p. 71; Fontana, pp. 90-1; U.S. ed., p. 63.
5. E. Rideau, op. cit., p. 324.   6. Ibid., pp. 325-6.

makes Christians sterile is that they do not love the world.[7]

Of course there is a sense in which Christians must *not* 'love the world'—the world of sinful pride and selfish ambition. But the world that is the creation of God—that we must love if we love its Creator. So this study of the spirituality of Teilhard de Chardin is no mere academic exercise. It is a summons and a challenge to us to continue the task he has so nobly initiated—the task of redeeming our generations for Christ. True, his teaching is at times obscure and his meaning difficult to elucidate. But of the inspiring power of that teaching and the general direction of his thought there can be no question. It might be summed up in one sentence:

By definition and principle it is the specific function of the Church to Christianize all that is human in man.[8]

We may then surely claim that Teilhard de Chardin expounds a 'faith for the twentieth century'. Without in any way wishing to water down the content of traditional Christianity, without surrendering a single principle of orthodox teaching, he sought to present that teaching enriched and deepened by the fertilization of ideas derived from his scientific vision. Just as, in the fifth century, Ambrose and Augustine interpreted Christian truth in terms of contemporary philosophical systems, just as in the thirteenth Aquinas reinterpreted that same truth in the light of Aristotelian metaphysics, so Teilhard in the twentieth century drew on the vast wealth of scientific lore to open men's minds still wider to the majesty of God and the appeal of Christ.

7. Ibid., pp. 326-7.
8. *The Future of Man*, p. 265; Fontana, p. 277.

Also available in the Fontana Religious Series

BY TEILHARD DE CHARDIN

The Phenomenon of Man
'What Teilhard has to say about the rise and development of
life is not only strict science, but pure poetry.'
Times Literary Supplement

Le Milieu Divin
'Will certainly take its place among the rare spiritual classics
of the twentieth century.'
The Times

The Future of Man
'Here we have creative thought . . . the reader cannot fail to
be inspired by these wonderful essays.'
Sunday Times

Hymn of the Universe
'A deeply religious work which must find a permanent place
in this treasury of mystical literature.'
Times Literary Supplement

Letters from a Traveller
'As travel literature these letters make dramatic reading. But
much more dramatic is the picture we have of the continuous
growth of his marvellous vision.'
Observer

About Teilhard de Chardin